ISBN: 0-97729
ISBN 13: 978-

You can visit us online at:

www.GrowingWithGrammar.com

Printed in the United States of America.

Ver. 2.0.0-4

Preface

For many years, I have been aware that educators around the world are in need of a thorough grammar program that can be used by anyone regardless of their background or beliefs. *Growing With Grammar* was developed to fill that need within the education community.

We have designed this thorough program to be user-friendly for both teacher and student by separating the subject matter into two books, the Student Manual and the Student Workbook (which includes a separate Answer Key). The Student Manual contains the learning portion of the subject matter, and the Student Workbook contains the hands-on portion which reinforces the lessons taught in the Student Manual. If desired, independent learners can work alone by utilizing the Student Manual and Student Workbook since the Answer Key is separate. To support each concept learned in the Student Manual, there is a corresponding workbook lesson. Review questions are integrated within each workbook lesson to constantly provide reinforcement of previous lessons learned. In addition, there are separate review lessons at the end of each chapter. There are 105 lessons in the Level 4 program which includes 8 review lessons.

Also, we have selected spiral binding for our books to ensure that they lie flat when open. The spiral binding on the workbook is at the top of the page to provide equal, unobstructed access for both right- and left-handed students.

Thank you for choosing *Growing With Grammar.* We look forward to the opportunity to provide you with the best tools possible to educate your children.

Table of Contents

Chapter 1-Growing With Sentences

Chapter 2-Growing With Nouns

Chapter 3-Growing With Pronouns

Chapter 4-Growing with Verbs

Chapter 5-Growing with Adjectives

Chapter 6-Growing with Adverbs

Chapter 7-Growing with Prepositions

Chapter 8-Growing with Words and Punctuation

Chapter 1

Growing with Sentences

1.1 Subjects and Predicates

Our basic unit of communication is the sentence. There are two main parts of a sentence: a **subject** and a **predicate**. Together, these two parts express a complete thought.

The **subject** part contains all the words that tell **who** or **what** the sentence is about and can consist of several words or just one word. This is called the **complete subject**.

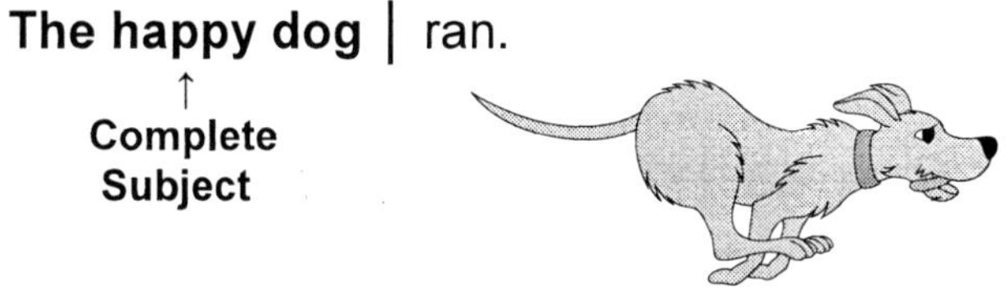

Samantha | saw a pack of wolves.
↑
Complete Subject

The **predicate** part contains all the words that tell what the subject is or does and can consist of several words or just one word. This is called the **complete predicate.**

The happy dog | **ran**.
↑
Complete Predicate

Samantha | **saw a pack of wolves**.
↑
Complete Predicate

As we have discussed, a sentence is a group of words expressing a complete thought. A sentence begins with a capital letter and ends with a period or other punctuation mark.

If a group of words does not express a complete thought, it is a **fragment** or only part of a sentence. Fragments can be turned into sentences by adding the missing words needed to express a complete thought.

Fragment: My Aunt Cherise.

What do we know about Aunt Cherise? How can this fragment be changed into a sentence? You need to add more words either to the subject section or the predicate section to complete the thought.

Words added to the subject section:	**I saw** my Aunt Cherise.
Words added to the predicate section:	My Aunt Cherise **went to Italy**.

More examples:

Fragment:	Went skating.
Words added to the subject section:	**The children** went skating.
Fragment:	The girls.
Words added to the predicate section:	The girls **made popcorn**.
Fragment:	On a trampoline.
Words added to the subject section:	**William jumped** on a trampoline.
Fragment:	Your glasses.
Words added to the predicate section:	Your glasses **are broken**.

1.2 Simple Subjects

The **simple subject** is the main word in the complete subject. It can be a **noun** or a **pronoun** and tells **who** or **what** the sentence is about.

As we have learned, the complete subject can be one word or several words. To figure out which word is the **simple subject**, you need to find the **noun** or **pronoun** that tells **who** or **what**.

A **mouse** | eats cheese.

The tiny gray **mouse** | is cute.

Who or what **eats cheese**? Who or what **is cute**?

In both of these sentences, the **simple subject** is the noun **mouse** since it tells **what** about both sentences.

More examples (with the simple subject in bold):

Jackson is a pitcher.

Camika wrote an essay.

The **shirt** is wrinkled.

The **monkey** climbed the tree.

Jacob broke his nose.

The **car** is blue.

The yellow **bird** flew from its cage.

My **dad** baked a pumpkin pie.

Lara bought apples.

The **canoe** is small.

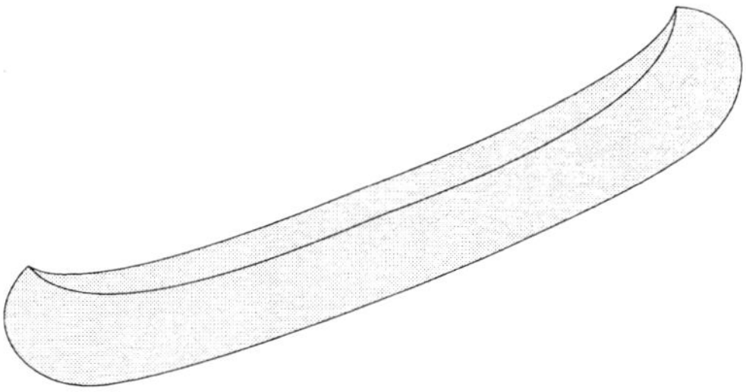

1.3 Simple Predicates

The **simple predicate** is the main word in the complete predicate. The simple predicate is a **verb** that tells what the subject **does** or **is**.

The complete predicate contains all of the words that say something about the subject. To figure out which part is the **simple predicate**, you need to find the **verb** in the sentence.

A mouse | **eats** cheese.

The tiny gray mouse | **is** cute.

The words **eats** and **is** are the **verbs** in these sentences. They are the **simple predicates**.

More examples (with the simple predicate in bold):

Jackson **is** a pitcher.

Camika **wrote** an essay.

The shirt **is** wrinkled.

The monkey **climbed** the tree.

Jacob **broke** his nose.

The car **is** blue.

The yellow bird **flew** from its cage.

My dad **baked** a pumpkin pie.

Lara **bought** apples.

The canoe **is** small.

1.4 Diagramming Simple Subjects and Predicates

A **sentence diagram** is a simple way of dividing a sentence into its basic parts. Many students find that they can understand a sentence better when they use a diagram.

Mom | **reads** the newspaper.

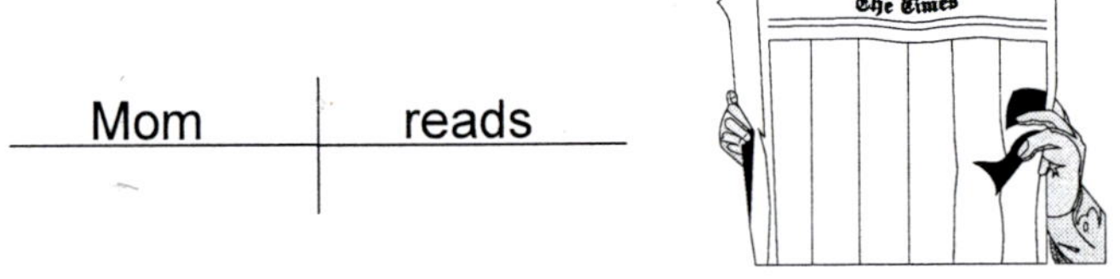

In a sentence diagram, the **simple subject** and **simple predicate** are placed on a horizontal line with the simple subject on the left, and the simple predicate on the right. A short vertical line divides the subject area from the predicate area.

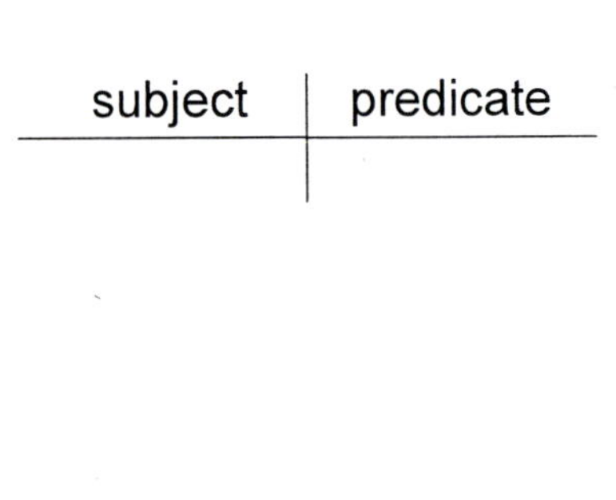

More examples:

The **boy kicked** the ball.

boy	kicked

He saves cans.

He	saves

Kristin asked a question.

Kristin	asked

The **cat chased** the mouse.

cat	chased

1.5 Compound Subjects and Predicates

You have learned how to identify the simple subject of a sentence. Some sentences, however, have two or more simple subjects that share the same predicate. This is called a **compound subject**. Compound subjects are joined by the conjunctions **and** or **or**. A **conjunction** is a word that joins other words or parts of a sentence together.

Isabella and **Nicholas** played.

Mom or **Dad** baked.

In the first sentence, the simple subjects are **Isabella** and **Nicholas**. They share the predicate **played**. In the second sentence, the simple subjects are **Mom** and **Dad**. They share the predicate **baked**.

More examples:

Caterpillars and **worms** crawl.

Barbara and **I** hiked.

Tony and **Donald** ate.

The **boys** and **girls** raced.

Just as a sentence can have a compound subject, it can also have a **compound predicate**. A compound predicate is two or more verbs in the sentence that tell what the subject is doing. The simple predicates in a compound predicate are usually joined by the conjunctions **and** or **or**.

Kate **swims** and **runs**.

Drew **hums** or **whistles**.

In the first sentence, the simple predicates are **swims** and **runs**. They tell what the subject **Kate** is doing. In the second sentence, the simple predicates are **hums** and **whistles**. They tell what the subject **Drew** is doing.

More examples:

The cat **eats** and **sleeps**.

Lamar **sat** and **talked**.

Squirrels **run** and **hide**.

Steve **cooked** and **cleaned**.

1.6 Diagramming Compound Subjects

To diagram a sentence with a **compound subject**, the simple subjects are placed on two horizontal lines, one above the other. The conjunction **and** or **or** is written on the dotted line that connects the two subject lines. A short vertical line divides the subject area from the predicate area, and the verb is placed on a line in the predicate area.

Sentences with a **compound subject** are diagrammed like this:

Isabella and **Nicholas** played.

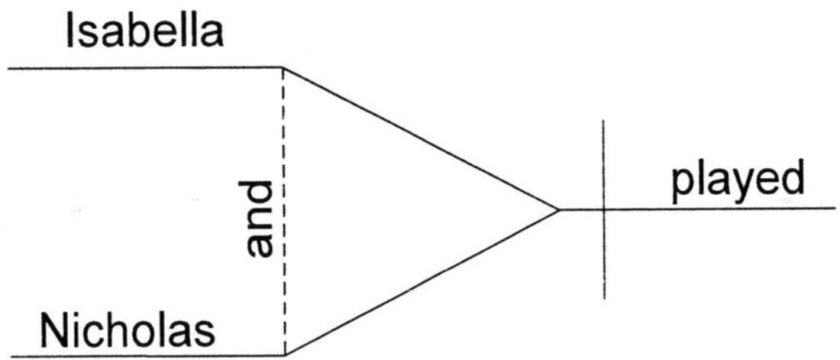

Mom or **Dad** baked.

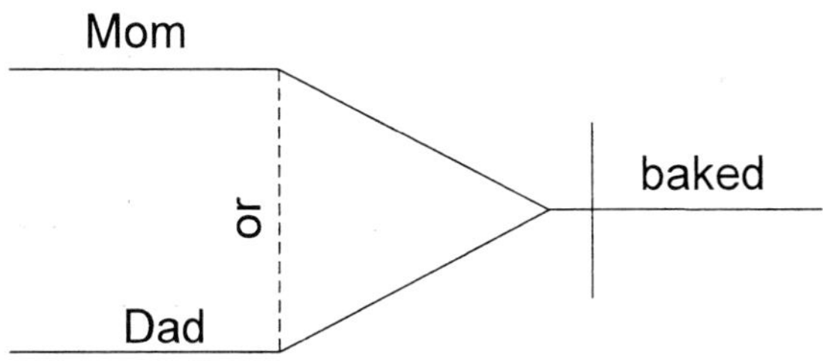

Patrick and **Everett** raced.

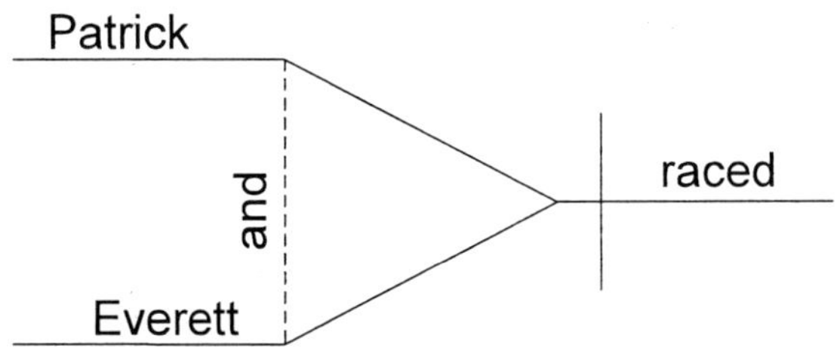

Jasmine or **Clayton** caught the spider.

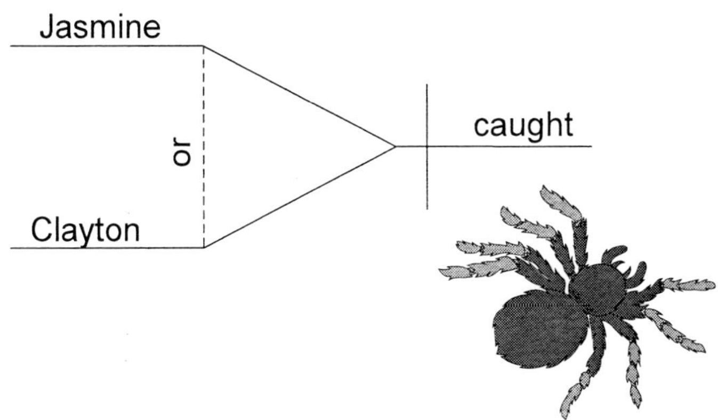

1.7 Diagramming Compound Predicates

To diagram a sentence with a **compound predicate**, place the subject on a horizontal line. A short vertical line is used to divide the subject area from the predicate area. The verbs are placed on two horizontal lines, one above the other. The conjunction **and** or **or** is written on the dotted line that connects the two predicate lines.

Sentences with a **compound predicate** are diagrammed like this:

Kate **swims** and **runs**.

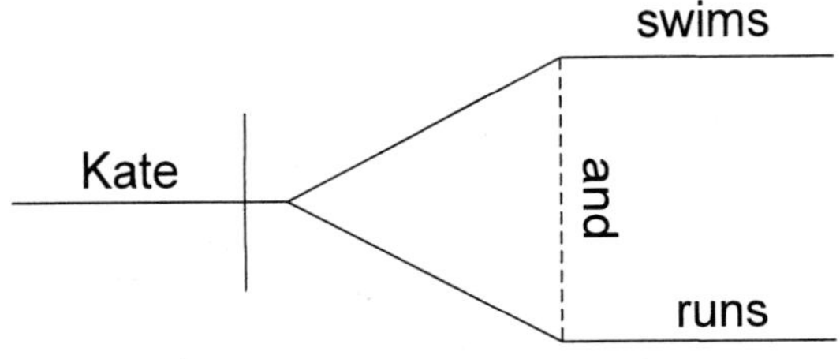

Drew **hums** or **whistles**.

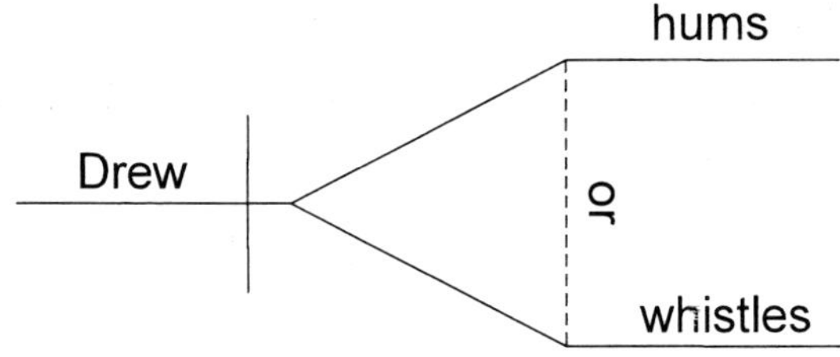

Deion **fishes** and **hikes.**

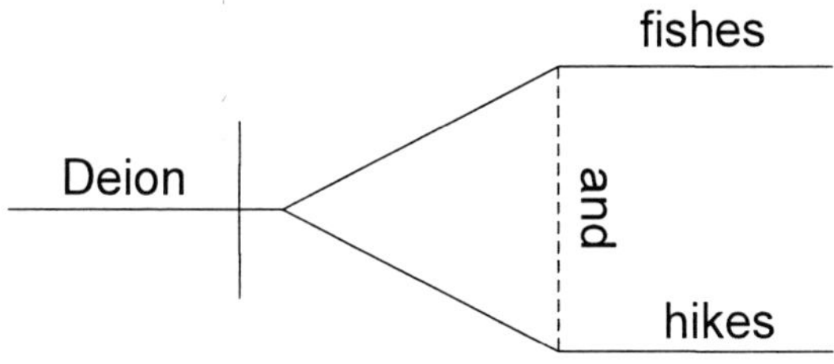

The deer **runs** and **jumps**.

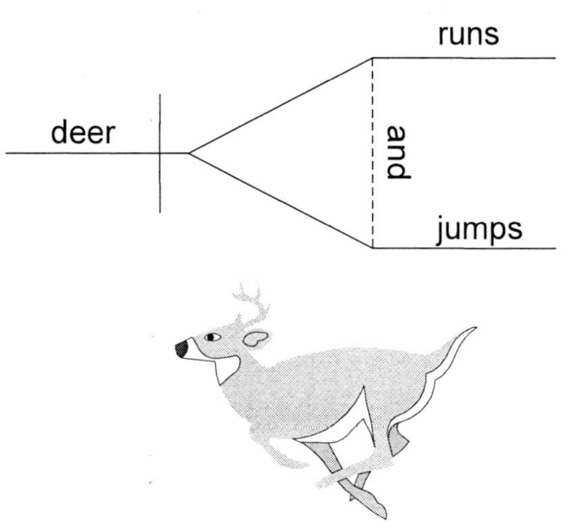

1.8 Combining Sentences

Sometimes we combine sentences to form a compound subject or compound predicate to keep our writing from being choppy.

Olivia climbed the tree. Ben climbed the tree.

These sentences are the same except for the subjects. The subjects can be combined to form one sentence that has a compound subject.

Olivia and **Ben** climbed the tree.

The compound subject in this sentence is made up of the two subjects **Olivia** and **Ben**, and joined by the word **and**. Both subjects share the verb **climbed**.

More examples:

Mario ate lunch. Jill ate lunch.

Mario and **Jill** ate lunch.

Keshia went to the zoo. Tevin went to the zoo.

Keshia and **Tevin** went to the zoo.

You can also combine sentences to form a compound predicate.

Charlotte fed her horse. Charlotte brushed her horse.

These sentences are the same except for the predicates. The predicates can be combined to form one sentence that has a compound predicate.

Charlotte **fed** and **brushed** her horse.

The compound predicate in this sentence is made up of the two verbs **fed** and **brushed**, and joined by the word **and**. Both predicates share the subject **Charlotte**.

More examples:

My sister hiked. My sister ran.

My sister **hiked** and **ran**.

The dog barks. The dog jumps.

The dog **barks** and **jumps**.

1.9 Two Subjects and Two Predicates

Some sentences have a **compound subject** and a **compound predicate**.

Zach and **Alexander** | **washed** and **waxed** the car.

In this sentence, the subjects are **Zach** and **Alexander**. The predicates are **washed** and **waxed**.

This sentence would be diagrammed like this:

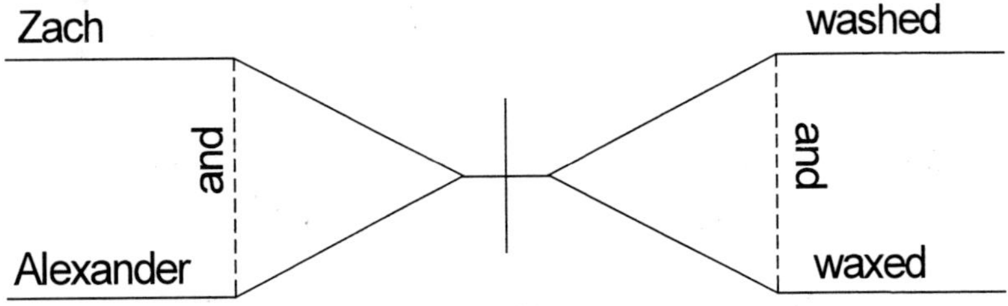

More examples:

Kristin and **Flora laughed** and **joked**.

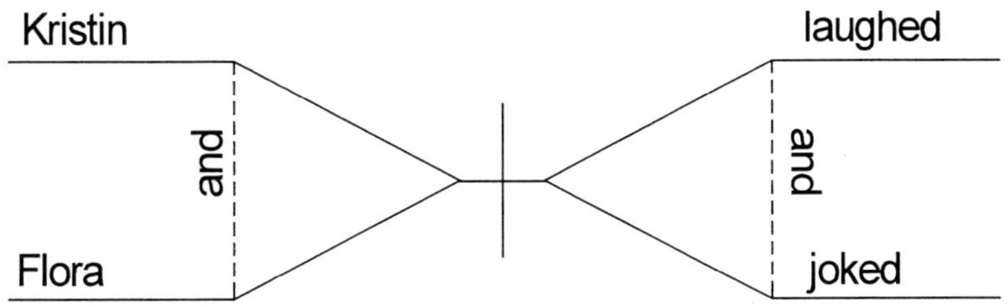

Bees and **wasps buzz** and **sting**.

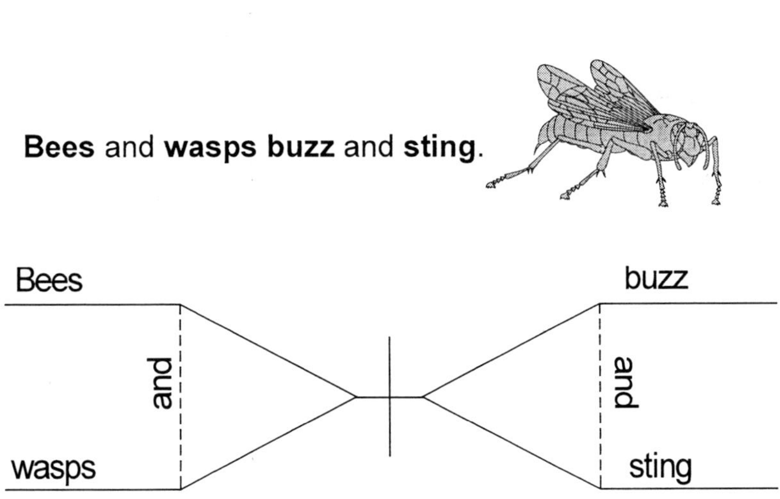

1.10 Run-on Sentences

A **run-on sentence** consists of two or more sentences that run together without correct punctuation to separate or join them.

Run-on: Dana showed us the gift Kiana gave it to her.

This sentence has two complete sentences that have been run together. A way to correct this sentence is to separate it into two sentences.

Correct: Dana showed us the gift. Kiana gave it to her.

Like the corrected sentence above, when two complete thoughts are joined, you can divide the sentence and punctuate it correctly.

More examples:

Run-on: Tia bought a radio for her car the car is black.

Correct: Tia bought a radio for her car. The car is black.

Run-on: Eli is in a wedding his sister is getting married.

Correct: Eli is in a wedding. His sister is getting married.

A run-on sentence can also occur when two related thoughts run together without a comma and a conjunction. Remember, conjunctions are words that join other words together.

Run-on: Amy paints pictures Liam sells them.

A way to correct this sentence is to turn it into a compound sentence. A **compound sentence** is two or more related simple sentences joined by a **coordinating conjunction** such as **and**, **but**, or **or**. A **comma** is placed before these joining words.

Correct: Amy paints pictures**, and** Liam sells them.

In the corrected sentence, the conjunction **and** separates the two thoughts while also showing a connection.

More examples:

Run-on: The cat is lost it ran away.

Correct: The cat is lost**, or** it ran away.

Run-on: Luke likes to surf he would rather ski.

Correct: Luke likes to surf**, but** he would rather ski.

1.11 Statements and Questions

There are four kinds of sentences. They are **statements**, **questions**, **commands**, and **exclamations**. Each kind requires a specific ending punctuation.

A **statement** tells something. It gives information and states a fact. A statement begins with a capital letter and ends with a period. A statement is sometimes called a **declarative** sentence.

Jared broke his finger.

The floor is sticky.

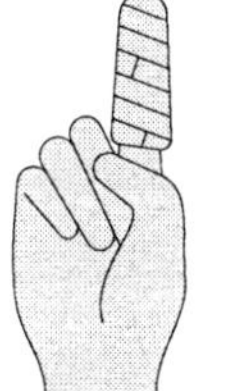

These sentences give information about **Jared's finger** and the **floor**. Both sentences begin with a capital letter and end with a period.

More examples:

The band played a song.

Lauren is eating breakfast.

Kristin ate an apple.

Garrick will walk home.

A **question** asks something and requires an answer. A question begins with a capital letter and ends with a question mark. A question is sometimes called an **interrogative** sentence.

Did Jared break his finger?

Is the floor sticky?

These sentences ask something about **Jared's finger** and the **floor**. They require an answer. Both sentences begin with a capital letter and end with a question mark.

More examples:

Did the band play a song?

Is Lauren eating breakfast?

Did Kristin eat an apple?

Will Garrick walk home?

1.12 Diagramming Questions

To diagram a question, you must find the subject and the predicate.

Did Gianna leave?

To find the subject in a **question**, rephrase the question as a statement. This will place the subject before the predicate (verb).

Gianna did leave.

The subject is **Gianna**. The predicate is the verb phrase **did leave**. A verb phrase contains more than one verb.

This question is diagrammed like this:

Did Gianna leave?

Gianna	Did leave

More examples:

Is Kylan reading?

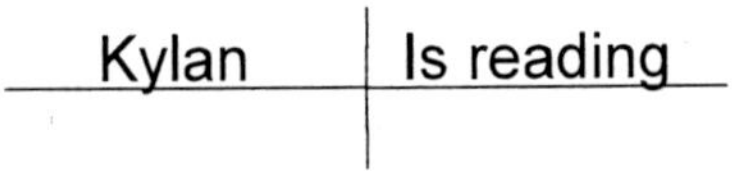

Kylan	Is reading

Can Andy sing?

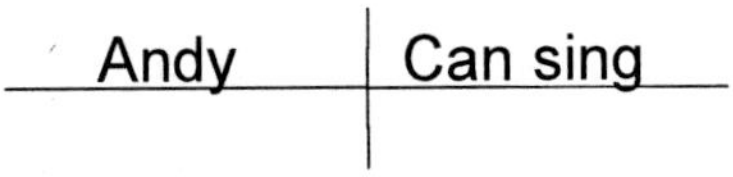

Andy	Can sing

Will you play?

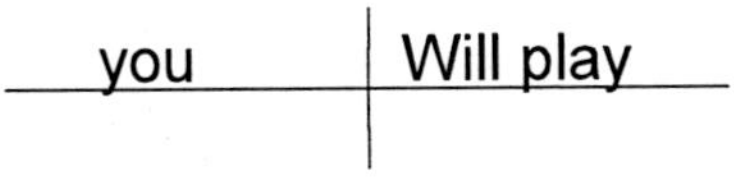

you	Will play

1.13 Commands and Exclamations

A **command** makes a request or tells you to do something. It is sometimes called an **imperative** sentence. A command begins with a capital letter and ends with a period, but can end with an exclamation mark if it shows strong feeling.

Clean the floor.

Clean the floor!

Both of these sentences are commands; however, the second sentence is a very strong command and is followed by an exclamation mark.

More examples:

Share the toy!

Wash the dishes.

Eat the banana.

Come home.

The subject of a command is always **you**, but it is not always spoken or written in the sentence.

(you) Clean the floor.

In this sentence, the subject is understood to be **you** even though it is not stated. We say that the subject **you** is understood.

More examples:

(you) Share the toy!

(you) Wash the dishes.

(you) Eat the banana.

(you) Come home.

An **exclamation** expresses strong feeling or emotion. An exclamation begins with a capital letter and ends with an exclamation mark.

Jared broke his finger!

The floor is sticky!

These sentences show strong feeling about the subjects. Both sentences begin with a capital letter and end with an exclamation mark.

More examples:

The stove is hot!

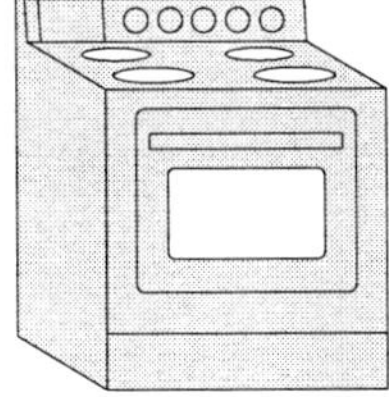

You won!

We did it!

That is amazing!

1.14 Diagramming Commands

To diagram a command, you must find the subject and the predicate.

Clean the floor.

As you have learned, in a command, the subject of the sentence is not always stated. The subject is **you** (understood).

(**you**) Clean the floor.

The subject in this sentence is **you** understood. The predicate is the verb **clean**.

This command is diagrammed like this:

Clean the floor.

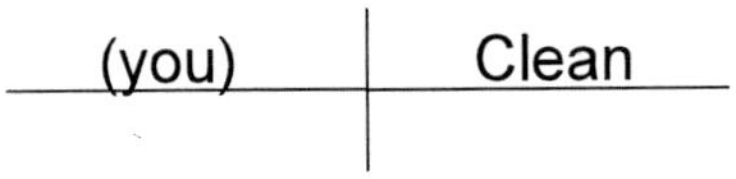

(you)	Clean

More examples:

Wash the dishes.

Share the toy.

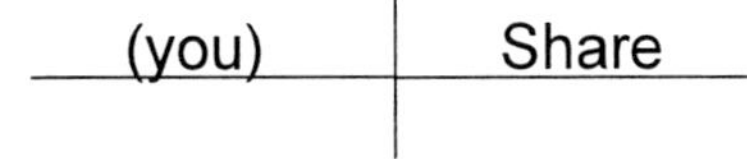

Eat the banana.

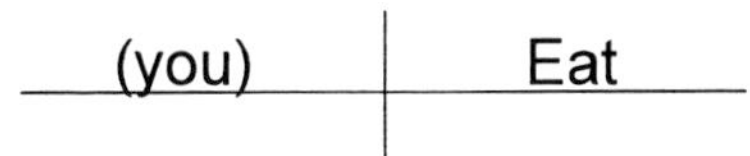

Come home.

Sometimes a command will include **you** and a name. This kind of command has a compound subject. This time **you** is stated and not understood.

You and Robin leave.

In this sentence, the subjects are **you** and **Robin**.

This type of command is diagrammed like this:

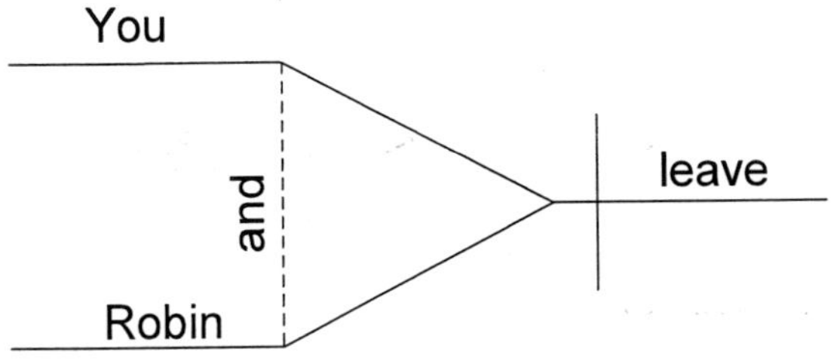

More examples:

You and Marcus wash the dishes.

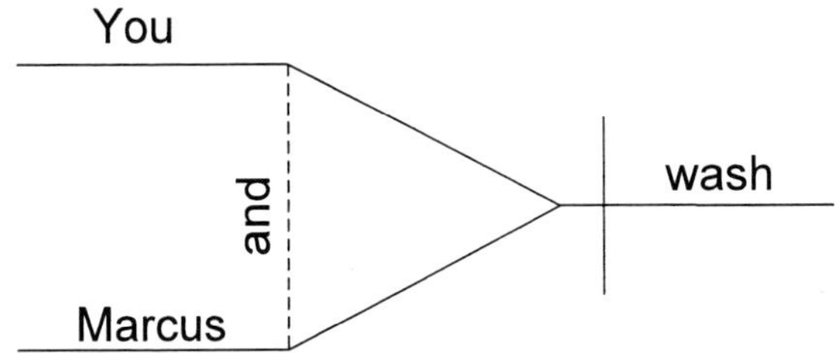

You and Emma share the toy.

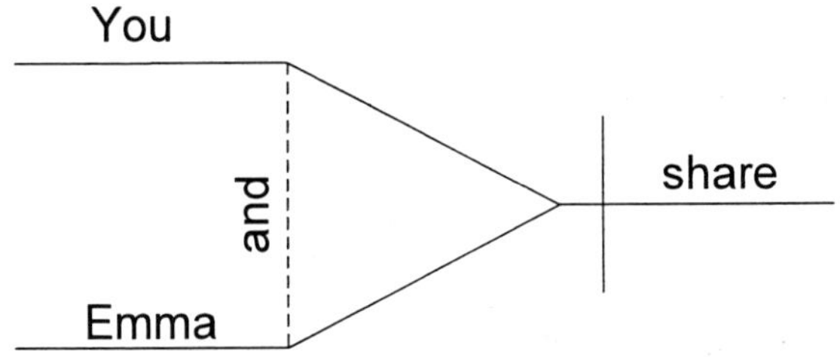

1.15 Direct Quotations

When people are talking to each other, it is called **dialogue**. There are two parts to written dialogue and they are the **speaker tag** and the **direct quotation**.

The **speaker tag** tells who is talking and how they said it.

Lucy said, “Mandy is the winner.”

“Is Mandy the winner?” **asked Lucy**.

In the first sentence, the speaker tag is **Lucy said**. In the second sentence, the speaker tag is **asked Lucy**. The speaker tags tell us that **Lucy** is the speaker in both sentences. These speaker tags also tell us how she said the sentences. In the first sentence she **said** something, and in the second sentence she **asked** something.

A **direct quotation** shows that someone is speaking and repeats the **exact** words that the person said.

When you include a direct quotation or dialogue in your writing, you should place **quotation marks** (" ") **before** and **after** the exact words of the speaker. A **comma** is used **before** the quotation when the speaker tag comes **first.** Also, the end punctuation goes **inside** the quotation marks.

Example: Lucy said**, "M**andy is the winner**."**

Notice that the first word of the quotation and the first word of the sentence are both capitalized.

When the speaker tag comes **last** in the sentence, a comma, question mark, or exclamation mark is used at the end of the quotation. This punctuation is placed **inside** the closing quotation marks. A period is used after the speaker's name.

"Mandy is the winner**,**" said Lucy**.**

"Mandy is the winner!" exclaimed Lucy**.**

"Is Mandy the winner**?**" asked Lucy**.**

When you include dialogue in your writing, make sure to indent and begin a new paragraph each time a different person speaks.

Example:

Lucy yelled, “Mandy is the winner of the marathon race!”

“Who came in second place?” asked Aunt Elizabeth.

“I think it was her best friend,” said Lucy.

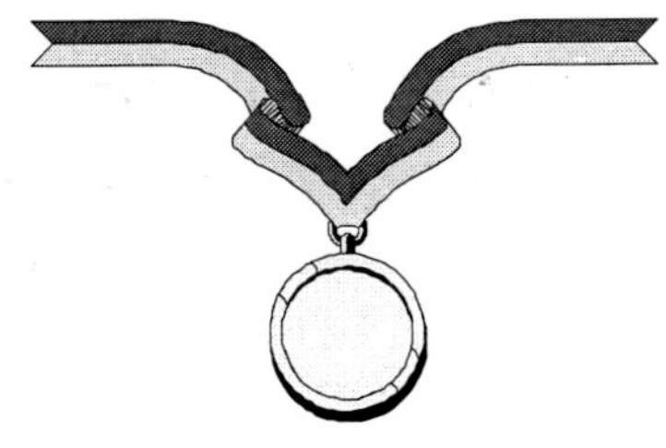

1.16 Indirect Quotations

Indirect quotations are not exact words but summaries of another person's words. Do not use quotation marks for indirect quotations.

Direct quote: Michael said, "I think it will rain."

Indirect quote: Michael said that he thinks it will rain.

In the first example, Michael's exact words are quoted. Quotation marks are used to show that it is a direct quotation. In the second example, Michael's words are summarized. No quotation marks are necessary for this **indirect quotation**.

More examples:

Direct quote: "The dog licked my face," said Carla.

Indirect quote: Carla said that the dog licked her face.

Direct quote: “Is the apple juicy?” asked Heidi.

Indirect quote: Heidi asked if the apple is juicy.

Direct quote: Elijah said, “I scored eight points.”

Indirect quote: Elijah said that he scored eight points.

Direct quote: “Has Nia arrived?” asked Tom.

Indirect quote: Tom asked if Nia has arrived.

1.17 Writing a Paragraph

A **paragraph** is a series of sentences about one topic or idea. A good paragraph includes a topic sentence, detail sentences, and logical order. The sentence that states the main idea of the paragraph is called the **topic sentence**. The other sentences describe and give more detail about the main idea. These are called the **detail sentences**.

There are three steps in writing a paragraph. The **first step** is to **plan** what the paragraph will be about. It is important to make sure the chosen topic is not too big. For example, if you wanted to write about holidays you would probably realize that you cannot cover the entire topic in one paragraph. You would then find that there are many smaller topics under the general topic of holidays.

Holidays: my favorite holiday
different types of holidays
holiday decorating
holiday traditions
holiday gift ideas

After the topic is chosen, you must decide what you want to say about it. Write down a few ideas about your topic.

Topic → my favorite holiday

Ideas: Independence Day
have fun decorating
cookout and good food
I have three sisters
fireworks
time spent with family

Look at your list of ideas. Do they all tell about the main topic? If not, then you should eliminate the ideas that don't. The idea **I have three sisters** does not have anything to do with the topic and should not be used.

You must put the main idea that you want to cover into a topic sentence. The **topic sentence** is usually found at the beginning of a paragraph, where it introduces the subject and tells what the paragraph will be about.

Example: Independence Day is my favorite holiday.

This topic sentence lets the reader know that the paragraph will be about a favorite holiday. Specifically, the paragraph will be about Independence Day and probably tell why it is a favorite holiday.

The **next step** is to **write** the paragraph. The first sentence of a paragraph should be indented. An indented sentence is one that is set in about half an inch from the left margin.

Put the ideas into sentences. Look at the order of the sentences and find a way that sounds best.

Example:

> Independence Day is my favorite holiday. My family has fun by decorating the house in patriotic colors. We have a cookout and eat delicious food. My family always sits together and watches fireworks at the park. *I am allergic to mosquitoes.* My favorite part of this holiday is the time my family spends together.

In this paragraph, the rest of the sentences, the detail sentences, give more information about the topic. However, be careful to include only sentences that discuss the main idea. There should be no unrelated sentences in your paragraph. The sentence **I am allergic to mosquitoes** has nothing to do with the topic and should not be in this paragraph.

Also, the sentences of the paragraph should be put in an order that will make sense to the reader.

Incorrect example:

> My family has fun by decorating the house in patriotic colors. My favorite part of this holiday is the time my family spends together. We have a cookout and eat delicious food. Independence Day is my favorite holiday. My family always sits together and watches fireworks at the park.

These sentences are not in the correct order, and this makes the paragraph difficult to understand.

Correct example:

> Independence Day is my favorite holiday. My family has fun by decorating the house in patriotic colors. We have a cookout and eat delicious food. My family always sits together and watches fireworks at the park. My favorite part of this holiday is the time my family spends together.

The **final step** is to **correct** any mistakes in your paragraph. Check to make sure you indented the first line, you started each sentence with a capital letter, you ended each sentence with the correct punctuation, and that you spelled each word correctly.

After you have finished your paragraph, you need to think of a title that will capture the reader's attention and summarize the information that appears in the paragraph. Be sure to capitalize the first word and all other important words in your title.

A fitting title for this paragraph might be **My Favorite Holiday**.

Chapter 1 Review

Subjects and Predicates: The **subject** contains all the words that tell **who** or **what** the sentence is about. The **predicate** contains all the words that tell what the subject is or does. If a group of words does not express a complete thought, it is a **fragment.**

Simple Subjects and Simple Predicates: The **simple subject** is the main noun or pronoun in the complete subject that tells **who** or **what** the sentence is about.

The **simple predicate** is the main verb in the complete predicate that tells what the subject **does** or **is**.

Sentence Diagramming: A sentence diagram starts with a horizontal line. The simple subject is placed on the left and the simple predicate on the right. A short vertical line divides them.

subject | predicate

Sentences with a **compound subject** are diagrammed like this:

Isabella and **Nicholas** played.

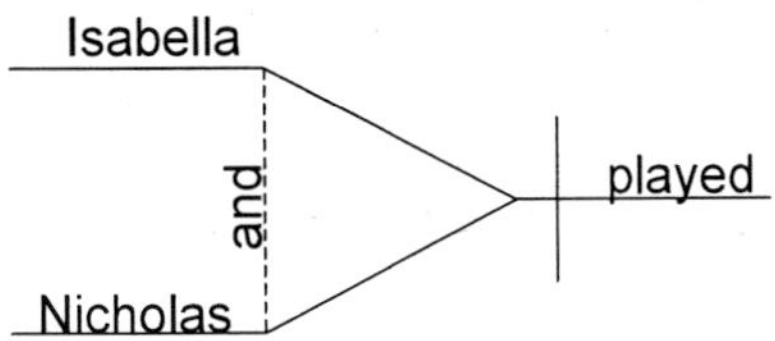

Sentences with a **compound predicate** are diagrammed like this:

Kate **swims** and **runs**.

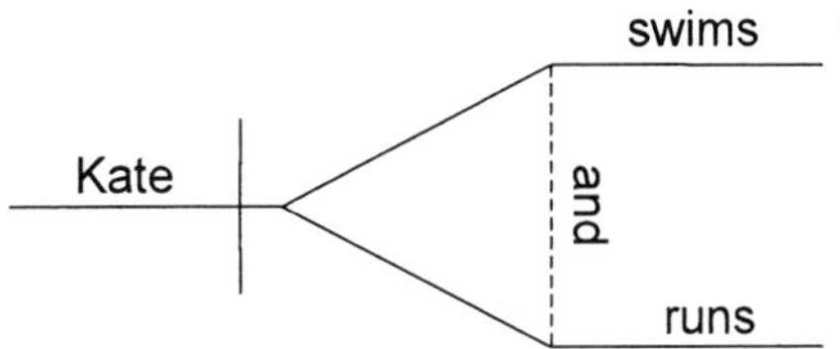

Sentences with a **compound subject** and a **compound predicate** are diagrammed like this:

Zach and **Alexander** **washed** and **waxed** the car.

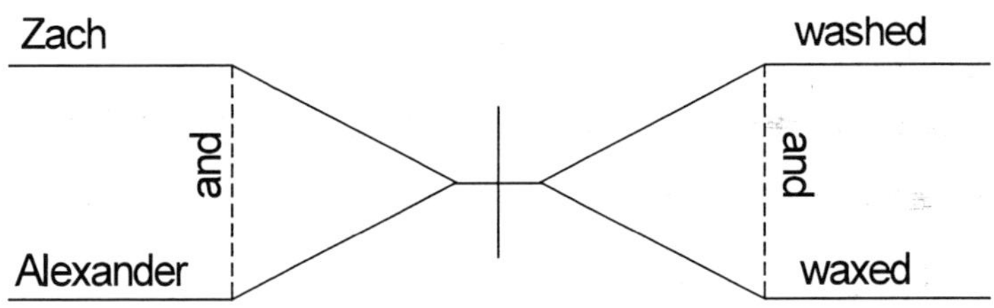

Run-on Sentences: A **run-on sentence** consists of two or more sentences that run together without correct punctuation to separate or join them.

Statements and Questions: A **statement** tells something. Statements begin with a capital letter, end with a period, and are sometimes called **declarative** sentences.

A **question** asks something and requires an answer. Questions begin with a capital letter, end with a question mark, and are sometimes called **interrogative** sentences.

Diagramming Questions: To find the subject in a **question**, you should rephrase the question as a statement. This will place the subject before the predicate (verb).

Did Gianna leave?

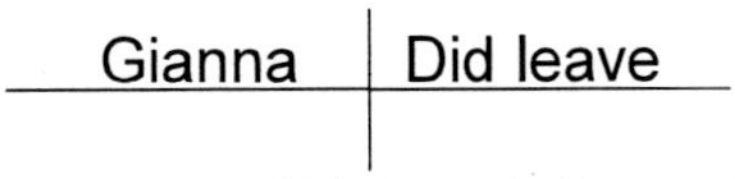

Gianna	Did leave

Commands and Exclamations: A **command** makes a request or tells you to do something. It is sometimes called an **imperative** sentence. A command begins with a capital letter and ends with a period, but can end with an exclamation mark if it shows strong feeling. In a command, we say that the subject **you** is understood.

An **exclamation** expresses strong feeling or emotion. An exclamation begins with a capital letter and ends with an exclamation mark.

Diagramming Commands: To diagram a command, you must find the subject and the predicate. The subject of a command is usually **you** (understood). A command is diagrammed like this:

Clean the floor.

Sometimes a command will include **you** and a name. This kind of command has a compound subject and **you** is stated and not understood. This type of command is diagrammed like this:

You and Robin leave.

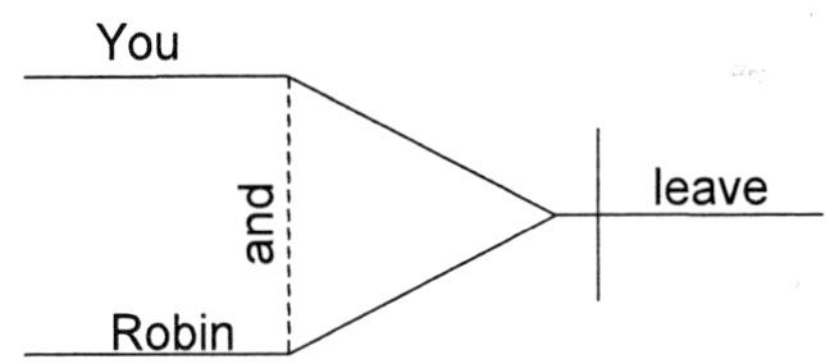

Direct Quotations: A **direct quotation** repeats the **exact** words that a person said. When you include a direct quotation or dialogue in your writing, you should place **quotation marks** (“ ”) **before** and **after** the exact words of the speaker.

-A comma is used before the quotation when the speaker tag comes first. Also, the end punctuation goes **inside** the quotation marks.

-When the speaker tag comes **last** in the sentence, a punctuation mark is used at the end of the quotation. The punctuation is placed **inside** the closing quotation marks, and a period is used after the speaker's name.

Indirect Quotations: **Indirect quotations** are not exact words but summaries of another person's words. Do not use quotation marks for indirect quotations.

Chapter 2

Growing With Nouns

2.1 Common Nouns and Proper Nouns

Nouns are naming words. A noun is the name of a **person**, **place**, or **thing**.

Person: man, neighbor, doctor

Place: basement, zoo, country

Thing: camera, truck, book

The **thing** category includes living things, nonliving things, ideas, feelings, and emotions.

Living things: dog, flower, bird

Nonliving things: rock, watch, rug

Ideas: joy, love, honesty

Nouns are divided into two groups: **common nouns** and **proper nouns**.

A **common noun** names **any** person, place, or thing. Common nouns are usually not capitalized unless they begin a sentence or are part of a title.

girl	state	dog
neighbor	country	day
artist	city	month
scientist	library	holiday

A **proper noun** is the **specific name** of a person, place, or thing. Begin the first word and every other important word in a proper noun with a capital letter.

Common Noun		**Proper Noun**
state	→	**C**alifornia
girl	→	**E**liza
dog	→	**S**pot
neighbor	→	**A**ndre **D**esmond
country	→	**M**exico
day	→	**T**uesday
artist	→	**P**ablo **P**icasso
city	→	**C**hicago
month	→	**O**ctober
scientist	→	**I**saac **N**ewton
library	→	**N**ew **Y**ork **P**ublic **L**ibrary
holiday	→	**M**other's **D**ay

2.2 Concrete and Abstract Nouns

Sometimes nouns are grouped into the categories **concrete** and **abstract**.

Concrete nouns are words that stand for things that you can **see**, **hear**, **smell**, **taste**, or **feel**.

uncle	statue	bird
man	house	cat
friend	beach	pencil

Most nouns are concrete nouns. The examples above are common nouns. Concrete nouns can also be proper nouns.

Uncle Bob	Liberty Bell	Polly

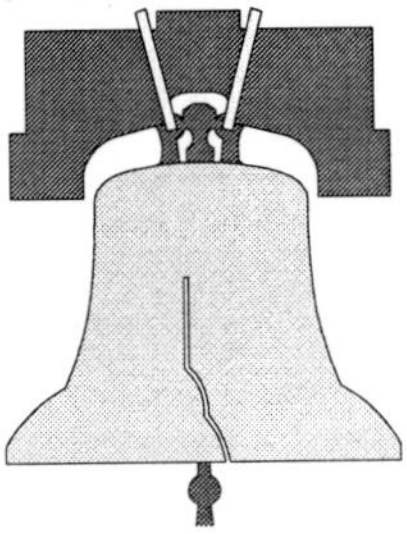

The opposite of a concrete noun is an **abstract noun**.

Abstract nouns are words that express things that you cannot experience by using your senses. You cannot **see**, **hear**, **smell**, **taste**, or **feel** them. They usually represent ideas, emotions, or qualities.

love	goodness	truth
bravery	time	honesty
pride	fear	loyalty
intelligence	anger	happiness
respect	friendship	curiosity
kindness	hope	joy
freedom	courage	success

If you cannot see the noun, it is most likely an abstract noun. Sometimes abstract nouns are called idea nouns.

2.3 Compound Nouns

Two or more words can be used together to form a single noun called a **compound noun**. Compound nouns can be written in different ways.

Compound nouns normally have two parts. These parts are sometimes written as one word.

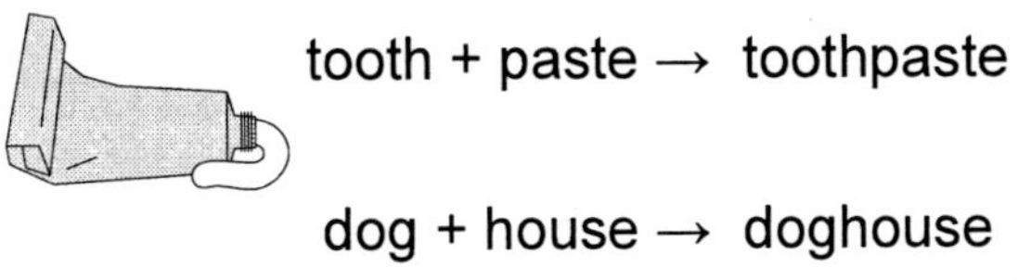

tooth + paste → toothpaste

dog + house → doghouse

Compound nouns usually have a different meaning than the two words when they are separate. In these examples, the words **tooth** and **paste** are two separate words, but when they are joined together they form the new word **toothpaste**. Also, the words **dog** and **house** are two separate words, but they become the new word **doghouse** when joined together.

More examples:

basket + ball → basketball

waste + basket → wastebasket

arm + chair → armchair

text + book → textbook

play + room → playroom

thunder + storm → thunderstorm

baby + sitter → babysitter

While some compound nouns are joined together to make one word, there are instances where compound nouns are written as two separate words.

full + moon → full moon

seat + belt → seat belt

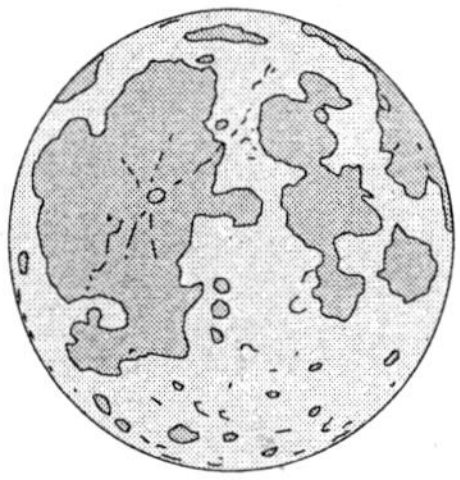

More examples:

police + officer → police officer

history + book → history book

fruit + juice → fruit juice

swimming + pool → swimming pool

light + switch → light switch

mountain + lion → mountain lion

Some compound nouns are written as hyphenated words.

great + grandfather → great-grandfather

hide + and + seek → hide-and-seek

More examples:

jack + in + the + box → jack-in-the-box

merry + go + round → merry-go-round

drive + in → drive-in

mother + in + law → mother-in-law

Check a dictionary if you are unsure how you should write each compound noun. If you cannot find the word in the dictionary, then write the noun as separate words.

2.4 Plural Nouns

Nouns can be **singular** or **plural**.

When a noun means **only one** person, place, or thing, it is said to be **singular**.

When a noun means **more than one** person, place, or thing, it is said to be **plural**.

Most nouns can be made plural just by adding **-s.**

lamp → lamp**s** pen → pen**s**

car → car**s** chair → chair**s**

flower → flower**s** cup → cup**s**

door → door**s** rock → rock**s**

kite → kite**s** star → star**s**

If a nouns ends in **s**, **ch**, **sh**, **x**, or **z**, add **-es** to form the plural noun.

class → class**es** wish → wish**es**

wax → wax**es** watch → watch**es**

buzz → buzz**es** coach → coach**es**

flash → flash**es** waltz → waltz**es**

Most nouns ending in a **vowel** and an **o** are made into a plural by adding **-s**.

stereo → stereo**s** yo-yo → yo-yo**s**

radio → radio**s** rodeo → rodeo**s**

cameo → cameo**s** patio → patio**s**

portfolio → portfolio**s** studio → studio**s**

Most nouns that end in a **consonant** and an **o** are made into a plural by adding **-es**.

hero → hero**es** echo → echo**es**

potato → potato**es** tomato → tomato**es**

veto → veto**es** mosquito → mosquito**es**

grotto → grotto**es** torpedo → torpedo**es**

Musical terms ending in **o** are an exception to this rule. These words require only an **-s** to form the plural.

piano → piano**s** soprano → soprano**s**

alto → alto**s** solo → solo**s**

cello → cello**s** banjo → banjo**s**

Check the dictionary if you are unsure how to write each plural noun. The letters **pl** stand for **plural** in a dictionary. When two choices are given for the plural, the first choice is usually preferred.

2.5 More Plural Nouns

Of course, not all plural nouns are formed simply by adding **-s** or **-es** to the singular noun. Here are some other ways to form **plural nouns**.

Some nouns end with a consonant letter and **y**. The plural is formed by changing the **y** to **i** and adding **-es**.

history → histor**ies**

story → stor**ies**

duty → dut**ies**

study → stud**ies**

city → cit**ies**

injury → injur**ies**

However, when the noun ends with a **vowel** and a **y,** the plural is made by adding **-s**.

play → play**s**

key → key**s**

chimney → chimney**s**

boy → boy**s**

donkey → donkey**s**

alley → alley**s**

Some nouns that end in **f** or **fe** are made plural by changing the **f** or **fe** to **-ves**.

scarf → scar**ves** calf → cal**ves**

life → li**ves** half → hal**ves**

wife → wi**ves** leaf → lea**ves**

For other nouns ending in **f** or **fe**, simply add **-s**.

roof → roof**s** chief → chief**s**

cliff → cliff**s** bluff → bluff**s**

belief → belief**s** reef → reef**s**

Check the dictionary if you are unsure how to write each plural noun. The letters **pl** stand for **plural** in a dictionary. When two choices are given for the plural, the first choice is usually preferred.

2.6 Irregular Plural Nouns

In order to form some plural nouns, you must change the spelling. These nouns are called **irregular plural nouns**.

one **man** → two **men**

one **goose** → three **geese**

The spelling of the nouns **man** and **goose** is changed to make the plural forms **men** and **geese**.

More examples:

woman → women

mouse → mice

tooth → teeth

louse → lice

foot → feet

person → people

child → children

ox → oxen

Some nouns do not change when they are used as plural.

one bison → seven bison

one fish → nine fish

one salmon → five salmon

one deer → four deer

one moose → two moose

one trout → two trout

one sheep → many sheep

one swine → six swine

Some nouns are always in the plural form but can be used as singular or plural.

one pair of scissors → two pairs of scissors

one pair of pants → three pairs of pants

one pair of pliers → four pairs of pliers

one pair of glasses → two pairs of glasses

2.7 Singular Possessive Nouns

A **singular possessive noun** is a word that shows ownership or possession by one person or thing. Possessive nouns are formed by adding an **apostrophe** and an **-s ('s)**.

the coat of the boy → the **boy's** coat

the ball that belongs to Ethan → **Ethan's** ball

Possessive nouns tell **whose**. **Whose** coat is it? It is the **boy's** coat. **Whose** ball is it? It is **Ethan's** ball.

The words **boy's** and **Ethan's** are possessive nouns. Each is made from a singular noun and shows that one person or thing owns something.

More examples:

the leaves of the tree → the **tree's** leaves

the name of the girl → the **girl's** name

the game that is owned by Damon → **Damon's** game

land that belongs to the farmer → the **farmer's** land

the friend of Pamela → **Pamela's** friend

a computer owned by Kendra → **Kendra's** computer

the puppy of the boy → the **boy's** puppy

a snorkel that belongs to a diver → a **diver's** snorkel

When a singular noun ends in **s**, you still add an **apostrophe** and an **-s ('s)** to show possession.

the fish that belongs to James → **James's** fish

the hem of the dress → the **dress's** hem

Notice that the words **James's** and **dress's** are singular possessive nouns even though they end in **s**. The possessive form was made by adding an **apostrophe** and an **-s ('s)**.

More examples:

the car that belongs to the boss → the **boss's** car

the boat that is owned by Ross → **Ross's** boat

the brother of Chris → **Chris's** brother

a script belonging to an actress → an **actress's** script

the needle of the compass → the **compass's** needle

the pencil of the waitress → the **waitress's** pencil

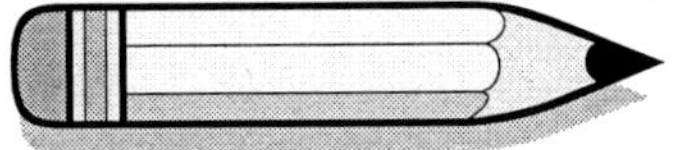

2.8 Plural Possessive Nouns

A **plural possessive noun** shows ownership by **more than one** person or thing. There are two rules to form plural possessive nouns.

First, for plural nouns that end in **s,** add an **apostrophe (').**

the maps belonging to the boys → the **boys'** maps

the nest shared by the birds → the **birds'** nest

The words **boys'** and **birds'** are plural possessive nouns. Each is made from a plural noun and shows that **more than one** person or thing owns something.

More examples:

the stickers belonging to the girls → the **girls'** stickers

the shoes owned by the clowns → the **clowns'** shoes

the toys of the babies → the **babies'** toys

a room shared by three sisters → the **sisters'** room

Second, for plural nouns that do **not** end in **-s**, add an **apostrophe** and **s ('s)**.

the coats owned by the men → the **men's** coats

the cheese shared by the mice → the **mice's** cheese

More examples:

the father of the children → the **children's** father

the hats owned by the women → the **women's** hats

the jobs the people have → the **people's** jobs

the eggs of the geese → the **geese's** eggs

2.9 Nouns of Direct Address

In a sentence, the name or title of the person being directly spoken to is called a **noun of direct address**.

Nouns of direct address are always proper nouns and are always capitalized. Commas are used to separate them from the rest of the sentence.

Tom, can you play?

Doctor, do I need stitches?

Tom is the name of the person being spoken to in the first sentence. In the second sentence, **Doctor** is the title of the person being spoken to. **Tom** and **Doctor** are both nouns of direct address and are followed by commas.

Nouns of direct address are set off by commas no matter where they are located in the sentence. They may be at the **beginning**, **end**, or **middle** of the sentence.

When the noun of direct address is located at the **beginning** of the sentence, a comma is used after the name.

Kevin, let me know when you are ready to leave.
Jada, where are you going?
Taylor, I think that you will win the race.
Mom, may I have a piece of cake?

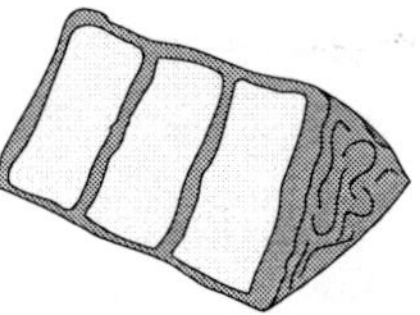

When the noun of direct address is located at the **end** of the sentence, a comma is used before the name.

Let me know when you are ready to leave**, Kevin**.
Where are you going**, Jada**?
I think that you will win the race**, Taylor**.
May I have a piece of cake**, Mom**?

When the noun of direct address is located in the **middle** of the sentence, commas are used before and after the name.

Let me know**, Kevin,** when you are ready to leave.
Where**, Jada,** are you going?
I think**, Taylor,** that you will win the race.
May I**, Mom,** have a piece of cake?

2.10 Noun Suffixes

A **suffix** is a letter or group of letters added to the **end** of a base word to make a new word. Suffixes usually change the meaning of the word.

Noun suffixes change some words into nouns. Some noun suffixes are **-er** and **-or**.

The suffix **-er** means **someone who** or **something that**.

sing + er = sing**er**

blend + er = blend**er**

The suffix **-er** at the end of the word **sing** means **someone who sings**. The suffix **-er** at the end of the word **blend** means **something that blends**.

More examples:

teach**er** = someone who teaches

work**er** = someone who works

camp**er** = someone who camps

record**er** = something that records

toast**er** = something that toasts

The suffix **-or** also means **someone who** or **something that**.

collect**or** = someone who collects

direct**or** = someone who directs

act**or** = someone who acts

connect**or** = something that connects

sail**or** = someone who sails

2.11 Dictionary Skills

The **dictionary** shows how to spell words and how to say them. It also tells the meanings of words.

The words in the dictionary are called **entry words** and are listed in **alphabetical order**.

To find a word in the dictionary, first look at the **guide words**.

Example
Guide words: **cab** **cadet**

The guide words are the words at the top of each page. The guide word on the left tells you the first word on the page, and the guide word on the right tells you the last word on the page. All other words on that page occur alphabetically between the two guide words.

Next, look at the **entry words**. The **entry words** are listed in the dictionary in alphabetical order.

The entry word **cactus** can be found in a dictionary with the guide words **cab** and **cadet.**

cactus (kăk-təs) any of a family of plants native to mostly dry regions that have succulent stems and branches with scales or spines instead of leaves

The letters in parentheses tell you how to pronounce the entry word **cactus**. The group of words after the parentheses is the definition that tells what the word means.

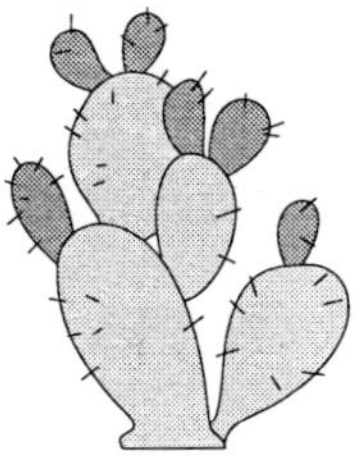

Sometimes there is more than one pronunciation for a word.

either (ē'thər, ī'thər) one or the other

Chapter 2 Review

Common Nouns and Proper Nouns: Common nouns name **any** person, place, or thing and are usually not capitalized unless they begin a sentence or are part of a title. **Proper nouns** are the **specific name** of a person, place, or thing and are usually capitalized.

Concrete and Abstract Nouns: **Concrete nouns** are nouns that you can **see**, **hear**, **smell**, **taste**, or **feel**. **Abstract nouns** are nouns that you cannot experience by using your senses. They usually represent ideas, emotions, or qualities.

Compound Nouns: Two or more words can be used together to form a single noun called a **compound noun** by joining the words, by using the words separately but together, or by placing a hyphen between the words.

Plural Nouns:

-Most nouns can be made plural just by adding **-s.**

-If a nouns ends in **s**, **ch**, **sh**, **x**, or **z**, add **-es**.

-For most nouns ending in a **vowel** and **o**, add **-s**.

-For most nouns ending in a **consonant** and **o**, add **-es**.

-Musical terms ending in **o** are an exception to this rule. They only need an **-s**.
-For nouns ending with a consonant letter and **y**, **c**hange the **y** to **i** and add **-es**. However, when the noun ends with a **vowel** and a **y,** add **-s**.
-For some nouns ending in **f** or **fe**, change the **f** or **fe** to **-ves**. For others ending in **f** or **fe**, simply add **-s**.

Irregular Plural Nouns: **Irregular plural nouns** have special spellings. Some nouns do not change when they are used as plural. Some nouns are always in the plural form but can be used as singular or plural.

Singular Possessive Nouns: A **singular possessive noun** shows ownership by one person or thing and is formed by adding an **apostrophe** and an **-s ('s)**. When a singular noun ends in **s**, add an **apostrophe** and an **-s ('s)** to show possession.

Plural Possessive Nouns: A **plural possessive noun** shows ownership by **more than one** person or thing and follows two rules.
-For plural nouns that end in **s,** add an **apostrophe (').**
-For plural nouns that do **not** end in **s**, add an **apostrophe** and **-s ('s)**.

<u>Nouns of Direct Address</u>: The name or title of the person being directly spoken to in a sentence is called a **noun of direct address**. They are always proper nouns and always capitalized. Commas are used to separate them from the rest of the sentence.

<u>Noun Suffixes</u>: A **suffix** is a letter or group of letters added to the **end** of a base word to make a new word. Suffixes usually change the meaning of the word. The suffixes **-er** and **-or** both mean **someone who** or **something that**.

<u>Dictionary Skills</u>: The **dictionary** shows how to spell words and how to say them. It also tells the meanings of the words.

-The **guide words** are the words that are at the top of each page.

-The **entry words** are listed in the dictionary in alphabetical order.

Chapter 3

Growing With Pronouns

3.1 Pronouns

A **pronoun** is a word that takes the place of one or more nouns. Pronouns are used the same way as the nouns they replace. Common pronouns include **I**, **you**, **he**, **she**, **it**, **we**, **they**, **me**, **her**, **him**, **us**, and **them**.

Jeremy is a gymnast. → **He** is a gymnast.

Bo and **Ed** went to the park. → **They** went to the park.

In the first sentence, the pronoun **he** replaces **Jeremy.** In the second sentence, the pronoun **they** replaces **Bo** and **Ed**.

Nouns are sometimes overused when writing. Instead of repeating the same noun over and over, you can use a **pronoun**.

Example:

Ron lost a new baseball. **Ron** was upset for a week. **Ron** finally found it under the bed.

In these sentences, the noun **Ron** is overused. The sentences would sound better if pronouns were used to replace some of the nouns.

Example:

Ron lost a new baseball. **He** was upset for a week. **He** finally found it under the bed.

Using pronouns in place of some of the nouns improves the sound of these sentences.

More examples:

Joe saved money to buy a skateboard **Joe** wanted.

↓

Joe saved money to buy a skateboard **he** wanted.

Tad and Sheri hoped **Tad and Sheri** were not late.

↓

Tad and Sheri hoped **they** were not late.

3.2 Subject and Object Pronouns

Pronouns that take the place of a noun or nouns in the subject part of a sentence are called **subject pronouns**.

The pronouns **I**, **you**, **he**, **she**, **it**, **we**, and **they** are used in the subject part of a sentence.

Naomi has the flu. → **She** has the flu.

The **play** starts at six o'clock. → **It** starts at six o'clock.

In the first sentence, the pronoun **she** replaces **Naomi.**
In the second sentence, the pronoun **it** replaces **play.**

More examples:
The **boy** made lunch. → **He** made lunch.

Rex and **Tina** went surfing. → **They** went surfing.

Grace and **I** drew pictures. → **We** drew pictures.

The **cat** chased the mouse. → **It** chased the mouse.

Pronouns that take the place of a noun or nouns in the predicate part of a sentence are called **object pronouns**.

The pronouns **me**, **you**, **him**, **her**, **it**, **us**, and **them** are used in the predicate part of a sentence.

The letter is from **Elizabeth**. → The letter is from **her**.

Rob smiled at **April** and **me**. → Rob smiled at **us**.

In the first sentence, the pronoun **her** replaces **Elizabeth.** In the second sentence, the pronoun **us** replaces **April** and **me**.

More examples:

Have you seen **Charles**? → Have you seen **him**?

I cleaned the **floor**. → I cleaned **it**.

Give these to **Calvin** and **Leo**. → Give these to **them**.

The cat belongs to **Skylar**. → The cat belongs to **her**.

3.3 Possessive Pronouns

Possessive pronouns take the place of possessive nouns. They show ownership or possession and never need apostrophes.

The pronouns **my**, **mine**, **your**, **yours**, **his**, **her**, **hers**, **its**, **our**, **ours**, **their**, and **theirs** are possessive pronouns.

Kamar's ball is white. → **His** ball is white.

That game belongs to **you**. → That game is **yours**.

In the first sentence, the possessive pronoun **his** replaces **Kamar's**. In the second sentence, the possessive pronoun **yours** replaces **you**.

More examples:

The **lion's** roar was loud. → **Its** roar was loud.

Nile's hair is blonde. → **His** hair is blonde.

The flowers belong to **us**. → The flowers are **ours**.

That story belongs to **Tyra**. → That story is **hers**.

Those paints belong to **you**. → Those are **your** paints.

Stacia and **Bart** own this car. → It is **their** car.

This is **my** house. → This house is **mine**.

Julia's mother is nice. → **Her** mother is nice.

This cat belongs to **you**. → This cat is **yours**.

The green tent belongs to **us**. → **Our** tent is green.

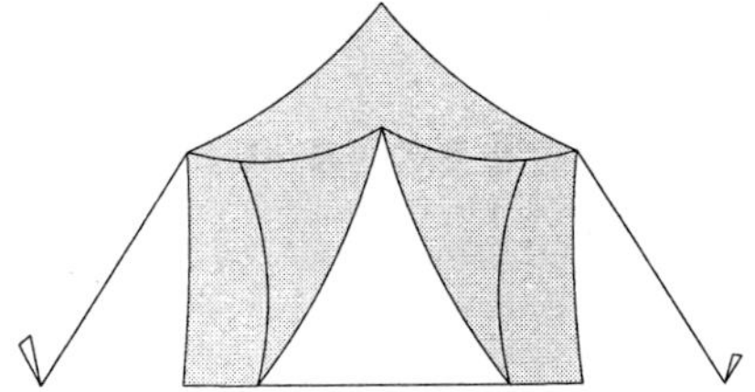

3.4 Personal Pronouns

Personal pronouns can be divided into three groups: **first person**, **second person**, and **third person**.

To replace the name of the person who is speaking, use **first person** pronouns. This includes the pronouns **I**, **me**, **my**, **mine**, **we**, **us**, **our**, and **ours**.

I found a dime in the yard.

That book is **mine**.

Our house is white

To replace the name of the person spoken to, use **second person** pronouns. This includes the pronouns **you**, **your**, and **yours**.

You found a dime in the yard.

That book is **yours.**

Your house is white.

To replace the name of the person, place, or thing we are speaking about, use **third person** pronouns. This includes the pronouns **he**, **him**, **his**, **she**, **her**, **hers**, **it**, **its**, **they**, **them**, **their**, and **theirs**.

He found a dime in the yard.

That book is **hers**.

Their house is white.

The noun or nouns that a pronoun refers to are called the **antecedent(s)**.

Charles washed **his** bike.

The **woman** lost **her** keys.

In the first sentence, **Charles** is the antecedent of the pronoun **his**. In the second sentence, **woman** is the antecedent of the pronoun **her**.

More examples:

Marco painted **his** bike.
↑ antecedent ↑ pronoun

The **bird** built **its** nest.
↑ antecedent ↑ pronoun

I ate lunch with **my** aunt.
↑ antecedent ↑ pronoun

Personal Pronouns

First Person	I, me, my, mine, we, us, our, ours
Second Person	you, your, yours
Third Person	he, him, his, she, her, hers, it, its, they, them, their, theirs

3.5 I or Me, We or Us

Pronouns are often used incorrectly, but they are actually easy to use. **I** is used in the subject and **me** is used after a verb.

I know the answer.

The water is too cold for **me**.

A common problem is deciding when to use **I** or **me** in a sentence with another subject.

Kevin and (**I** or **me**) played chess today.

Which pronoun is correct? The easiest way to figure this out is to think of the sentence as two sentences. Then decide what pronoun you would use if the other subject was not there. When you add the other subject, do not change the form of the pronoun.

Separate into two sentences: Kevin played chess today.

I played chess today.

-or-

Me played chess today.

I is the correct pronoun for this sentence.

The answer: Kevin and **I** played chess today.

Another example:

Joseph waved at Gabrielle and (**I** or **me**).

Separate into two sentences: Joseph waved at Gabrielle.

Joseph waved at **I**.

-or-

Joseph waved at **me**.

The answer: Joseph waved at Gabrielle and **me**.

The pronouns **we** and **us** sometimes cause trouble. Remember to use **we** in the subject and **us** after a verb.

We know the answer.

The water is too cold for **us**.

A common problem is deciding when to use **we** or **us** in a sentence with another subject.

Joshua and (**we** or **us**) climbed the hill.

Which pronoun is correct? As we just learned, think of the sentence as two sentences and choose the correct pronoun.

Separate into two sentences: Joshua climbed the hill.

We climbed the hill.

-or-

Us climbed the hill.

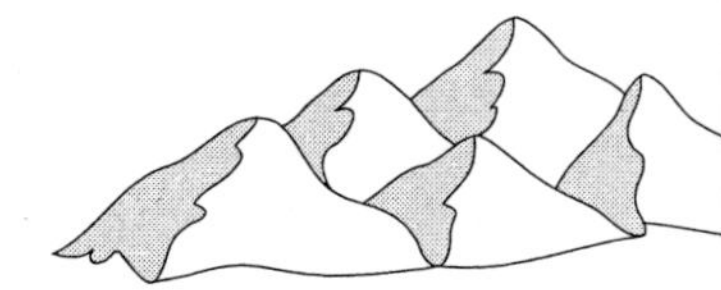

We is the correct pronoun for this sentence.

The answer: Joshua and **we** climbed the hill.

Another example:

He was mad at Emily and (**we** or **us**).

Separate into two sentences: He was mad at Emily.

He was mad at **we**.

-or-

He was mad at **us**.

The answer: He was mad at Emily and **us**.

Another thing to remember is to always name yourself last when you are talking about another person and yourself.

Incorrect: **I** and Trevan went to the store.

This sentence is incorrect, and doesn't sound right either. Remember that the other person always comes first.

Correct: Trevan and **I** went to the store.

More examples:

Incorrect: Mom helped **me** and Brenna.

Correct: Mom helped Brenna and **me**.

Incorrect: The ice cream is for **us** and Chantal.

Correct: The ice cream is for Chantal and **us**.

Incorrect: **We** and Kylan rode on the tractor.

Correct: Kylan and **we** rode on the tractor.

3.6 Using Pronouns Correctly

The antecedent of a pronoun should always be clearly understood. Remember, the **antecedent** is the noun or nouns to which a pronoun refers.

Do not use a pronoun if the reference is unclear because this can cause the sentence to be confusing.

Unclear: Leanne asked Joan a question. **She** did not know the answer.

Who didn't know the answer? This sentence needs to be changed to make the meaning clear. A pronoun should not be used here.

Clear: Leanne asked Joan a question. **Joan** did not know the answer.

More examples:

Unclear: I saw an eagle and a hawk in the sky. **It** flew fast. (What flew fast?)

Clear: I saw an eagle and a hawk in the sky. The **eagle** flew fast.

Unclear: Gina and Rhonda cleaned **her** bedroom.
(They cleaned whose bedroom?)

Clear: Gina and Rhonda cleaned **Gina's** bedroom.

Example (with a clear pronoun reference):

John played with his dog, and **it** barked.

Using a pronoun is appropriate in this sentence since the pronoun **it** clearly refers to the noun **dog**.

Remember, pronouns are used to take the place of nouns. Do not use both a noun and a pronoun as the subject of a sentence.

Incorrect: The **boys they** picked apples.
Correct: The **boys** picked apples.
Correct: **They** picked apples.

Incorrect: **Johanna she** was waiting for me.
Correct: **Johanna** was waiting for me.
Correct: **She** was waiting for me.

3.7 Capitalization

A person's **name** is a proper noun. Each part of a **name** including the **first**, **middle**, and **last** names should be capitalized.

Carol **M**arie **D**owns   **B**lake **R**yan **W**illiams

Initials that take the place of a person's name are always capitalized and should be followed by a period.

Cedric **A**. Parker   **D**. **F**. Seymour

Titles of respect that are used before a person's name are capitalized.

Mr. Johnson	**M**rs. Green	**M**iss Nolan
Doctor Jarvis	**A**unt Celia	**U**ncle Isaac
Grandma Rose	**C**hief Carlson	**P**rofessor Chang
President Adams	**S**enator Scott	**K**ing Edward

The pronoun **I** is always capitalized.

Do you think **I** will win first prize?

Most **geographical** and **place names** are proper nouns and should be capitalized.

Streets, **Roads**, **and Highways:**

Canyon **D**rive	**E**merson **A**venue	**M**ain **S**treet
U.**S**. **H**ighway 36	**M**ichigan **R**oad	**M**aple **L**ane

Cities, **States**, **and Provinces:**

Baltimore	**L**ondon	**M**adrid	**T**okyo
Kansas	**O**regon	**Q**uebec	**N**ova **S**cotia

Countries and Continents:

Argentina	**C**hina	**I**reland	**E**gypt
Antarctica	**E**urope	**A**sia	**A**frica

Islands, **Mountains**, **Deserts**, **and Bodies of Water:**

Canary **I**slands	**R**ocky **M**ountains	**S**ahara **D**esert
Amazon **R**iver	**L**ake **G**eneva	**P**acific **O**cean

Parks and Dams:

Yellowstone **N**ational **P**ark

Banff **N**ational **P**ark

Grand **C**oulee **D**am

Hoover **D**am

Buildings, Structures, and Monuments:

Empire **S**tate **B**uilding

Great **W**all of **C**hina

Golden **G**ate **B**ridge

Lincoln **M**emorial

Planets and Stars:

Mars

Saturn

Venus

Jupiter

Big **D**ipper

Milky **W**ay

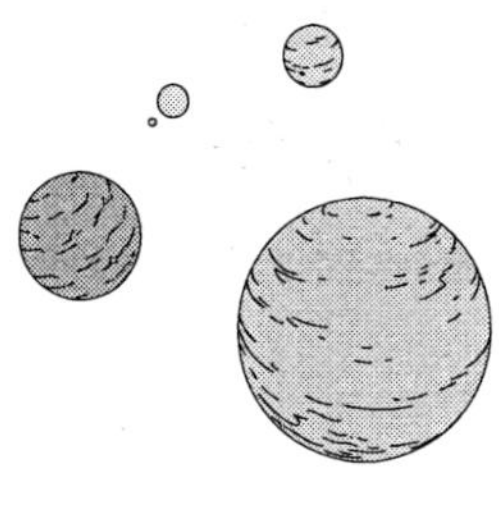

3.8 Capitalizing Groups, Events, and Days

The specific names of **various groups** should be capitalized. Notice that only the **important words** of a name are capitalized. Unimportant words, like the **of** in Metropolitan Museum **of** Art, are not capitalized.

Businesses, Stores, and Restaurants:

Ted's **T**ire **C**ompany	**A**my's **C**andy **S**hop
Digger's **S**hovel **S**tore	**S**ancho's **M**exican **R**estaurant

Organizations, Clubs, and Institutions:

Marietta **T**ennis **C**lub	**R**ed **C**ross
National **F**ootball **L**eague	**C**hicago **S**ymphony

Schools, Libraries, and Hospitals:

Franklin **E**lementary **S**chool	**P**rinceton **U**niversity
Toronto **P**ublic **L**ibrary	**P**roctor **H**ospital

The names of historical and special events, periods of time, calendar items, and historical documents should be capitalized.

Historical Events and Periods of Time:

World **W**ar II	**F**rench **R**evolution
the **M**iddle **A**ges	the **R**enaissance

Historical Documents:

Gettysburg **A**ddress	**M**agna **C**arta
Bill of **R**ights	**M**ayflower **C**ompact

Special Events:

Thanksgiving **D**ay **P**arade	**S**uper **B**owl
Boston **M**arathon	**G**reenfield **A**rt **S**how

Calendar Items:

Wednesday	**S**aturday	**N**ovember
Mother's **D**ay	**F**lag **D**ay	**V**alentine's **D**ay

Names of specific nationalities, languages, and religious references are capitalized.

Nationalities and Languages:

Chinese **C**anadian **S**wiss **I**talian

French **P**ortuguese **K**orean **S**panish

Religious References:

Judaism **C**hristianity **H**induism **B**uddhism

God **T**orah **I**slam **B**rahma

Koran **B**ible **J**ewish **C**atholic

3.9 More Capitalization

Names of specific ships, trains, and aircraft should be capitalized.

Ships:

Mayflower	**C**utty **S**ark	**S**anta **M**aria

Trains:

Orient **E**xpress	**F**lying **S**cotsman	**B**ullet **T**rain

Aircraft:

Spirit of **S**t. **L**ouis	**M**emphis **B**elle	**A**ir **F**orce **O**ne

Brand names of business products should be capitalized but not the product.

Nestlé chocolate	**D**isney movie	**L**evi's jeans
Microsoft software	**H**einz ketchup	**F**ord truck

Capitalize the **first word**, **last word**, and all **important words** in the **titles** of books, newspapers, magazines, and poems. Do not capitalize **a**, **an**, **the**, **and**, **but**, or other **short words** unless they are the first or last word in a title.

Books:

A **D**ay at **G**randma's **H**ouse

Harry and **H**is **D**og

Newspapers:

Charleston **N**ews and **R**eview

Danville **J**ournal **S**tar

Magazines:

American **M**ountain **C**limber

Baseball **E**nthusiast

Poems:

A **W**inter **N**ight

Fun in the **S**un

Capitalize the **first word** in a sentence, a direct quote, a line of poetry, a greeting of a letter, and the closing of a letter.

Sentence:

My umbrella is yellow.

The pencil was on the floor.

Direct Quote:

Pieter said, "**M**y family loves to collect stamps."

"**H**ave you seen my jacket?" asked Molly.

Poetry:

Roses are red,

  Grass stains are green.

Your pants are dirty,

  They used to be clean.

Greeting of a Letter:

Dear Aunt Mary,

Dear Mr. Thompson,

Closing of a Letter:

Yours truly,

Sincerely yours,

3.10 Words that Are Not Capitalized

There are some words that should **not** be capitalized.

Do not capitalize the **seasons**.

spring summer fall / autumn winter

Do not capitalize **directions**.

south west north east

Do not capitalize a **career choice** unless it is used as a title.

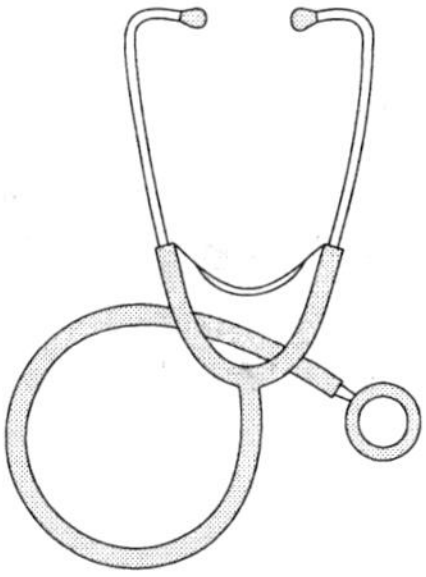

Harold is a **doctor**.

Today I will be seeing **Doctor** Harold.

Do not capitalize a **school subject** unless it is a language or has a number after it.

My favorite subject is **history**.

I love my **Spanish** class.

Next year I will be taking **Chemistry 1**.

Do not capitalize the following types of words.

Do not capitalize **plants**.

violets grass elm tree rose

Do not capitalize **diseases**.

mumps measles polio flu

Do not capitalize **games**.

marbles checkers dominoes tag

Do not capitalize **foods**.

waffles oranges apple pie corn

Do not capitalize **animals**.

elephant beaver lion dachshund

Do not capitalize **musical instruments**.

horn tuba flute drums

However, if the word is preceded by the name of a country, then capitalize the **country name only**.

Examples:

We planted **African** violets in our yard.

My cousin was sick with **German** measles.

We love to play **Chinese** checkers.

My mother made **Belgian** waffles for breakfast.

Sally has an **Australian** shepherd puppy.

My brother is learning to play the **French** horn.

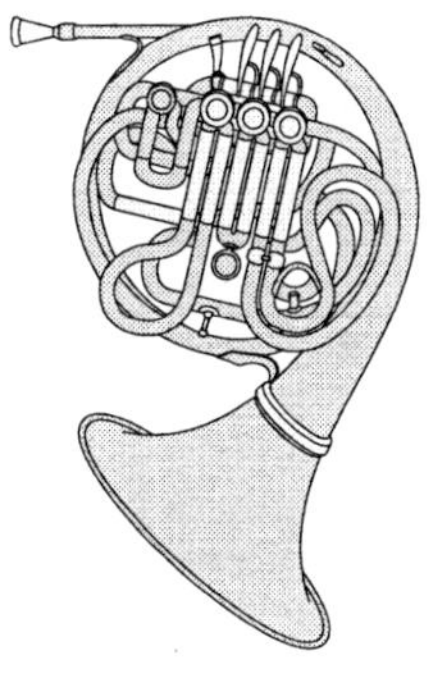

3.11 Giving Directions

It is often necessary to give **directions** to someone to tell them how to do something, how to get from one place to another, or how to make something.

Directions need to be in order to make proper sense. Some words that are used to help write directions in order are called time order words. These are words like **first**, **second**, **third**, **next**, **last**, **before**, **then**, **finally**, and **after**.

These words can be used to tell someone how to follow a recipe.

Example:
To make a s'more treat at an outdoor campfire, **first**, place a marshmallow on a stick and roast it over the fire until it is brown. **Second**, place the marshmallow on a graham cracker. **Third**, add a small piece of chocolate on top of the marshmallow. **Finally**, place another graham cracker on top.

If the steps are out of order, the recipe might not turn out properly.

Incorrect example:

Add a small piece of chocolate on the marshmallow. Place a marshmallow on a graham cracker. Roast the marshmallow over a fire until it is brown. Add another graham cracker on top.

These steps are out of order. Roasting the marshmallow after it is been placed on the graham cracker could be difficult. The s'more treat would not turn out the way it is supposed to.

Time order words can also be used to tell someone how to get to a certain place. It is important that the directions are in the proper order and also specific.

Not very specific: To get to the bank you can turn right at the stop sign. Turn left at the next street. Then walk down the street until you see the bank.

Specific: To get to the bank, **first**, turn right on Adams Street. **Next**, turn left on Main Street. **Finally**, walk for two blocks until you see the bank on the left side of the street.

Chapter 3 Review

Pronouns: A **pronoun** takes the place of one or more nouns. Common pronouns include **I**, **you**, **he**, **she**, **it**, **we**, **they**, **me**, **her**, **him**, **us**, and **them**.

Possessive Pronouns: **Possessive pronouns** show ownership and never need apostrophes. They are words like **my**, **mine**, **your**, **yours**, **his**, **her**, **hers**, **its**, **our**, **ours**, **their**, and **theirs**.

Personal Pronouns: First person pronouns are **I**, **me**, **my**, **mine**, **we**, **us**, **our**, and **ours**. Second person pronouns are **you**, **your**, and **yours**. Third person pronouns are **he**, **him**, **his**, **she**, **her**, **hers**, **it**, **its**, **they**, **them**, **their**, and **theirs**.

I or Me, We or Us: The easiest way to decide whether to use **I** or **me** in a sentence is to think of the sentence as two sentences. Then decide what pronoun you would use if the noun were not there. When you add the noun, do not change the form of the pronoun. Do the same for deciding between **we** and **us**.

Rules for Capitalization:

-Each part of a **name**

-**Initials**

-**Titles** of respect

-The pronoun **I**

-Most **geographical** and **place names**

-The specific names of **various groups**

-Names of specific **nationalities**, **languages**, and **religious references**

-Names of specific **ships**, **trains**, and **aircraft**

-**Brand names**

-The **first**, **last**, and all **important words** in **titles**

-The **first word** in a sentence, a direct quote, a line of poetry, the greeting of a letter, and the closing of a letter

Words That Are Not Capitalized: Do not capitalize seasons, directions, career choices, school subjects, plants, diseases, musical instruments, foods, animals, or games.

Chapter 4

Growing with Verbs

4.1 Action Verbs

Action verbs are words that tell what action the subject of a sentence is doing. In a sentence, the most important part of the predicate is the verb.

Annelies **reads** poetry.

Nathan **writes** plays.

The action verbs **reads** and **writes** tell what action the subjects **Annelies** and **Nathan** are performing.

More examples:

Diane **paints** the fence.

The children **sing** songs.

Dashiell **rides** his bike.

Kevin **draws** animals.

Most action verbs talk about actions we can see like **jumping** or **working**. However, action verbs may also represent actions that take place but cannot easily be seen.

Joshua **forgot** his shoes.

Ethan **enjoys** baseball.

The action verbs **forgot** and **enjoys** tell what action the subjects **Joshua** and **Ethan** are performing, but they are actions that cannot be seen.

More examples:

We **learned** this song.

I **appreciate** your help.

Mom **likes** chocolate.

Do you **trust** me?

4.2 Direct Objects

The noun or pronoun that receives the direct action of the verb is called the **direct object**. The verb used with a direct object is always an action verb.

Sarah knits **sweaters**.

Matthias helped **Sandra**.

To identify the direct object, say the subject and verb followed by **what** or **whom**.

Sarah **knits what** or **whom**? **Sweaters** answers the question and is the direct object in the first sentence. Matthias **helped what** or **whom**? **Sandra** answers the question and is the direct object in the second sentence.

More examples (with the direct object in bold):
Alyson hugged **Bradyn**.

Arden rode a **bike**.

The dentist examined my **teeth**.

Here is how a sentence with a direct object is diagrammed.

subject	predicate	**direct object**

The direct object is placed on the same line with the subject and predicate. It is separated from the predicate by a short vertical line that does not break through the horizontal line.

More examples:

Alyson hugged Bradyn.

Alyson	hugged	**Bradyn**

Arden rode a bike.

Arden	rode	**bike**

The dentist examined my teeth.

dentist	examined	**teeth**

Not every sentence has a direct object. If nothing answers the question **what** or **whom**, then there is **no** direct object.

Brenna danced today.

Kristin sang beautifully.

Brenna danced **what** or **whom**? Nothing answers this question. There is no direct object. The word **today** tells **when** Brenna danced. It does not answer the question **what** or **whom**. Kristin sang **what** or **whom**? Again, there is no answer to this question. The word **beautifully** tells **how** Kristin sang and does not answer the question what or whom.

More examples with no direct object:

The fish jumped.

The boy ran quickly.

The dog barked.

She whispered softly.

4.3 Linking Verbs

There are verbs that do not show action or tell what the subject is doing. These verbs tell what the subject is by linking the subject to a word in the predicate that names or describes it. These are called **linking verbs** and they are the main verb in the sentence.

That man **is** a coach.

She **was** my friend.

In the first sentence, the linking verb **is** connects the subject **man** to the word **coach**. In the second sentence, **was** is the linking verb. It connects the subject **she** to the word **friend**.

.

The most common linking verbs are forms of **be**.

am **is** **are** **was** **were**

There are rules for using these forms of the verb **be**.

Use **am** and **was** with the pronoun **I**.

I am afraid.

I was finished.

Use **are** and **were** with the pronoun **you**.

You are sweet.

You were late.

Use **is** or **was** with other **singular** subjects.

He is my cousin.

Joy is my friend.

The **floor was** wet.

The **window was** shut.

Use **are** or **were** with the **plural** subjects.

We are soccer players.

The **boys are** eight years old.

They were happy.

The **ants were** active.

4.4 Predicate Nouns

A **predicate noun** is a word that follows a linking verb and renames the subject of the sentence.

That man is a **coach**.

She was my **friend**.

In the first sentence, **coach** is a predicate noun because it is a noun that follows the linking verb **is** and renames the subject **man**. In the second sentence, **friend** is a predicate noun because it is a noun that follows the linking verb **was** and renames the subject **she**.

More examples (with the predicate noun in bold):

That bird is a **cardinal**.

Lisa is my **cousin**.

They were **gymnasts**.

My parents are **farmers**.

On a diagram, the predicate noun is placed on the same line with the subject and predicate. It is separated from the predicate by a short diagonal line that does not break through the horizontal line.

That bird is a **cardinal**.

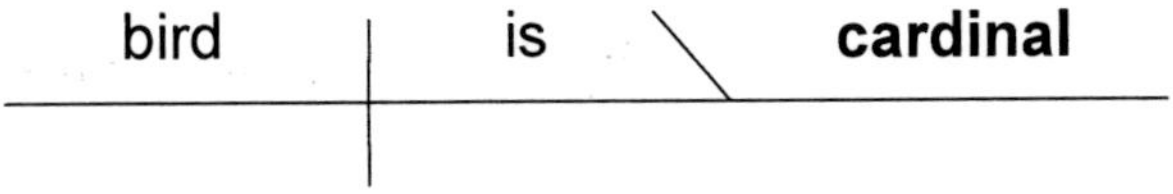

bird | is \ **cardinal**

Lisa is my **cousin**.

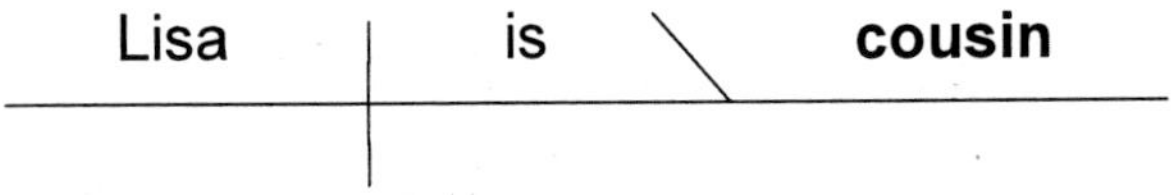

Lisa | is \ **cousin**

They were **gymnasts**.

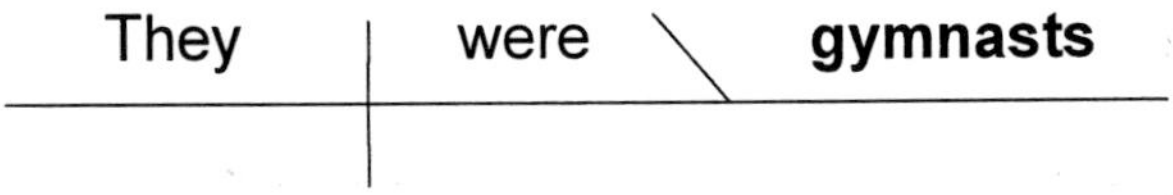

They | were \ **gymnasts**

My parents are **farmers**.

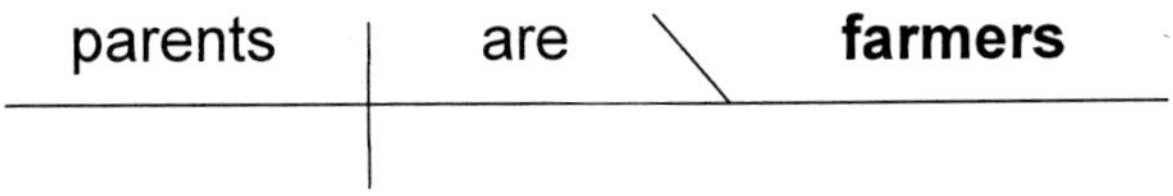

parents | are \ **farmers**

4.5 Contractions Formed with Not

A **contraction** is a word made by combining two other words. The words are combined and some letters are dropped. The letters that are dropped are replaced by an **apostrophe (')**.

Some contractions are formed by combining the word **not** with a **verb**.

do + not = **don't** is + not = **isn't** can + not = **can't**

In these examples, the verbs **do**, **is**, and **can** have been combined with the word **not** to form contractions. The apostrophe takes place of the letter **o** in **not**.

More examples:

are + not = aren't were + not = weren't

was + not = wasn't has + not = hasn't

have + not = haven't had + not = hadn't

does + not = doesn't did + not = didn't

will + not = won't should + not = shouldn't

would + not = wouldn't must + not = mustn't

can + not = can't could + not = couldn't

Be sure to use **doesn't** and **don't** correctly.

Doesn't is used with **singular subjects**

Incorrect: He don't know the answer.

Correct: He **doesn't** know the answer.

More examples:

Maria doesn't want to eat her spinach.

The **boy doesn't** need a ride.

Mom doesn't like rude behavior.

Don't is used with **plural subjects** and the pronouns **I** and **you**.

Incorrect: They doesn't know that song.

Correct: They **don't** know that song.

More examples:

You don't have your jacket on.

I don't know how to get there.

The **children don't** want to leave.

4.6 Contractions Formed with Pronouns

Some contractions are formed by combining a **pronoun** with a **verb**.

I + will = **I'll** we + will = **we'll** you + will = **you'll**

In these examples, the pronouns **I**, **we**, and **you** have been combined with the verb **will** to form contractions. The apostrophe takes the place of the letters **w** and **i** in **will**.

More examples:

Contractions formed with the pronoun **you**:

you are → you're	you will → you'll
you have → you've	you would → you'd

Contractions formed with the pronoun **I**:

I am → I'm	I will → I'll
I have → I've	I would → I'd

Contractions formed with the pronoun **we**:

we are → we're	we will → we'll
we have → we've	we would → we'd

Contractions formed with the pronoun **it**:

it is → it's	it will → it'll
it has → it's	it would → it'd

Contractions formed with the pronoun **he**:

he is → he's	he will → he'll
he has → he's	he would → he'd

Contractions formed with the pronoun **she**:

she is → she's	she will → she'll
she has → she's	she would → she'd

Contractions formed with the pronoun **they**:

they are → they're	they will → they'll
they have → they've	they would → they'd

4.7 Helping Verbs

A **helping verb** is a verb that helps another verb. It comes before the main verb to tell about the action. Helping verbs are sometimes called **auxiliary verbs**.

Mara **has made** cookies.

David **can help** us.

In these sentences, the words **has** and **can** are helping verbs to the main verbs **made** and **help**.

More examples:

Dakota **will wrap** the gift.

I **have seen** two foxes.

She **is going** home.

We **did watch** the parade.

You **should wait** for her.

Helping verbs

Try to memorize these 23 helping verbs.

am	have	do	shall	may
is	has	does	will	might
are	had	did	should	must
was			would	can
were				could
be				
being				
been				

Sometimes a verb can have **more than one** helping verb.

John **will be using** the computer.

We **have been fishing**.

In the first sentence, **will** and **be** are the helping verbs to the main verb **using**. In the second sentence, **have** and **been** are the helping verbs to the main verb **fishing**.

More examples:

My sister **might be sleeping**.

He **has been eating** lunch.

You **could have invited** Andy.

I **will be planting** a garden.

We **should have gone** with Mom.

Some verbs can be used as a helping verb or as a main verb in a sentence.

Helping verb: He **is helping** my friend.

Main verb: He **is** my friend.

Helping verb: I **was working** as a gardener

Main verb: I **was** a gardener.

.

Helping verb: I **am singing**.

Main verb: I **am** a singer.

4.8 Verb Phrases

A **verb phrase** contains a main verb plus one or more helping verbs. The main verb is the last word in the verb phrase.

We **have learned** our math facts.

Jody **can play** the clarinet.

In these sentences, the verb phrases are **have learned** and **can play**. The main verbs are **learned** and **play**.

More examples:

I **can buy** an ice cream cone.

You **should clean** your bedroom.

Mom **was feeling** ill.

Jacob **is going** to basketball practice.

Verb phrases can have more than one helping verb.

We **might be playing** baseball.

↑ ↑

two helping verbs

You **should have been waiting** patiently.

In these sentences, the verb phrases are **might be playing** and **should have been waiting**. The main verbs are **playing** and **waiting**.

More examples:

The boys **will be arriving** soon.

John **had been working** all morning.

Dan **might have been sleeping**.

Tara **could have been swimming** today.

Questions should be changed to statements to find the verb phrase.

Can you find my keys?

You **can find** my keys.

The verb phrase is **can find**. Changing the question into a statement makes the verb phrase easier to find.

More examples:

Did you eat breakfast?

You **did eat** breakfast.

Has Jamar been painting the fence?

Jamar **has been painting** the fence.

Have you cleaned your room?

You **have cleaned** your room.

Although the word **not** can be found between a helping verb and a main verb in a sentence, it is not a verb or part of the verb phrase. The **contraction** form of not is never part of the verb phrase, either.

Charlie has **not** finished his lunch.

It did**n't** rain today.

In these sentences, the verb phrases are **has finished** and **did rain**.

More examples (with the verb phrase underlined):

I have **not** made my bed.

Tyrell will **not** answer my question.

Emily is**n't** talking to me.

You should**n't** play in the street.

4.9 Verb Tenses

Verbs tell if something is happening now, if it will happen later, or if it has already happened. This is called the **tense** of a verb. Tense tells when the action occurred or will occur.

Present Tense

Verbs that show what is happening now are said to be in the **present tense**. If the subject is **singular** or the pronouns **he**, **she**, or **it**, then add **-s** to the verb to show present tense.

He **makes** the sandwiches.

The dog **jumps** the fence.

She **swims** fast.

Do not add an **-s** to verb when the subjects are **plural** or the pronouns **I**, **you**, **we**, or **they**.

I **eat** the sandwiches.

We **jump** the fence.

The girls **swim** fast.

Some verbs end with a **consonant letter** followed by a **y**. Change the **y** to **i** and add **-es.**

The bird **flies** south.

Dad **worries** about us.

Future Tense

Verbs that tell about something that has not happened yet are called **future tense**. The future tense is formed by using **will** or **shall** before the verb. **Shall** and **will** are used with the pronouns **I** and **we**. For all other nouns and pronouns, only use **will**.

I **shall wash** the clothes.

She **will fold** the clothes.

Past Tense

Verbs that tell what has already happened are called **past tense**. To form the past tense of most verbs, add **-ed** to the verb.

jump → jump**ed** talk → talk**ed**

For some verbs that end with **e**, drop the **e** and add **-ed**.

save → sav**ed** race → rac**ed** arrive → arriv**ed**

Some verbs end with a **consonant letter** and a **y**. Change the **y** to **i** and add **-ed**.

carry → carr**ied** try → tr**ied** bury → bur**ied**

Some verbs end with a **single vowel** followed by a **single consonant**. **Double the final consonant** and add **-ed**.

hop → hop**ped** dip → dip**ped** wrap → wrap**ped**

Here are more examples of verbs in **present**, **past**, and **future tense**.

Present	**Past**	**Future**
laugh	laughed	will laugh
love	loved	will love
cry	cried	will cry
stop	stopped	will stop

Progressive verb tenses show **continuing action** in the **present**, **past**, and **future**.

Examples: I am learning. → *present*
I was learning. → *past*
I will be learning.→ *future*

The **progressive verb tense** shows if the **action is happening**, **was happening**, or **will be happening**.

The **present progressive tense verb** is formed by combining **am**, **is**, or **are** with the **-ing** form of a **verb**.

Example: I **am** sleeping.
She **is** sleeping.
You **are** sleeping.

The **present progressive tense verb** tells that the **action** is **happening** or **continuing in the present**. In these examples, the **action** of **sleeping** is **happening now**.

The **past progressive tense verb** is formed by combining **was** or **were** with the **-ing** form of a **verb**.

Example: I **was** sleeping.
You **were** sleeping.

The **past progressive tense verb** tells that the **action was happening** or **continuing in the past**. In these examples, the **action** of **sleeping** was **happening** at some time in the **past**.

The **future progressive tense verb** is formed by combining **will be** with the **-ing** form of a **verb**.

Example: I **will be** sleeping.

The **future progressive tense verb** tells that the **action will be happening** or **continuing in the future**. In this example, the **action** of **sleeping will be occurring** at some time in the **future**.

4.10 Irregular Verbs

The past tense of most verbs is made by adding **-ed**. However, some verbs are irregular verbs. An **irregular verb** is one that does not form its past tense by adding **-ed**. Instead, you must change the spelling of these verbs to form the past tense, and it is usually best to memorize these forms.

Today you **feel** ill.
Yesterday you **felt** well.

Today I **tell** a joke.
Yesterday I **told** a story.

The spelling of the irregular verbs **feel** and **tell** are changed to form the past tense forms **felt** and **told**.

More examples:

sing → sang leave → left

run → ran lose → lost

come → came grow → grew

know → knew bite → bit

hide → hid	slide → slid
sting → stung	swing → swung
fall → fell	weep → wept
build → built	win → won
hold → held	think → thought
see → saw	go → went
bring → brought	send → sent
sit → sat	pay → paid
say → said	lead → led

4.11 Using Irregular Verbs

Sometimes we use the helping verbs **has**, **have**, or **had** with past tense irregular verbs.

For some irregular verbs, the past tense without a helping verb is the same as the past tense with a helping verb.

I **tell** a joke.

I **told** a story.

I **have told** a story.

Verb	**Past** without helping verb	**Past** with helping verb has, have, or had
teach	taught	taught
catch	caught	caught
buy	bought	bought
stand	stood	stood
keep	kept	kept
sleep	slept	slept
spend	spent	spent
fight	fought	fought
wind	wound	wound

make	made	made
meet	met	met
bring	brought	brought
say	said	said
sit	sat	sat
leave	left	left
lose	lost	lost
build	built	built
win	won	won
hold	held	held

Other irregular verbs have different past forms. One is used without a helping verb. The other is used with the helping verbs **has**, **have**, or **had**.

We **speak** to Mom.

We **spoke** to Mom.

We **have spoken** to Mom.

Verb	**Past** without helping verb	**Past** with helping verb has, have, or had
draw	drew	drawn
run	ran	run
throw	threw	thrown
begin	began	begun
get	got	gotten
see	saw	seen
eat	ate	eaten
sing	sang	sung
grow	grew	grown
come	came	come
give	gave	given
ring	rang	rung
know	knew	known
break	broke	broken
tear	tore	torn
write	wrote	written
wear	wore	worn
ride	rode	ridden
bite	bit	bitten
freeze	froze	frozen
go	went	gone

4.12 Subject – Verb Agreement

In a sentence, the verb must agree with the subject in order to make sense. A singular subject must have a singular verb, and a plural subject must have a plural verb.

If the subject of the sentence is **singular** or is the pronoun **he**, **she**, or **it**, then add an -**s** to the verb. This is called the -**s form** of the verb. Verbs in the present tense frequently end with -**s**.

Incorrect: The horse gallop two miles.

Correct: The **horse gallops** two miles.

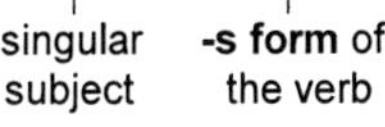

Incorrect: She examine fossils.

Correct: **She examines** fossils.

↑ singular subject ↑ -**s form** of the verb

If the subject of the sentence is **plural** or is the pronoun **I**, **you**, **we**, or **they**, then do not add **-s** to the verb. This is called the **plain form** of the verb.

Incorrect: The horses gallops two miles.

Correct: The **horses gallop** two miles.

↑ plural subject ↑ **plain form** of the verb

Incorrect: They examines fossils.

Correct: **They examine** fossils.

↑ plural subject ↑ **plain form** of the verb

More examples:

Alexander answers the question.

The **boys answer** the question.

Cecile lives in Saskatchewan.

We live in Saskatchewan.

The **hen lays** eggs.

Many **hens lay** eggs.

He runs three miles.

I run three miles.

Dad pays the telephone bill.

You pay the telephone bill.

Stella lands the airplane.

The **pilots land** the airplane.

The **boy paints** beautiful pictures.

The **boys paint** beautiful pictures.

The **dog chases** the cat.

The **dogs chase** the cat.

4.13 The Verb Have

Have is an irregular verb that shows that somebody owns something and can be used as a **main verb**. **Have** and its forms **has** and **had** can also be used as helping verbs.

When used alone, **have**, **has**, or **had** is the main verb in the sentence. **Have** and **has** are the present tense forms of the verb.

If the subject is **I**, **you**, **we**, **they**, or is **plural**, use the verb **have.**

They have a pet goat.

You have an ear infection.

Octagons have eight sides.

If the subject is **he**, **she**, **it**, or is **singular**, use the verb **has**.

She has a present for Tony.

It has a red collar.

The **car has** new brakes.

Had is the **past tense** form of the verb **have** and can be used with **singular** or **plural** subjects.

Jack had a turkey sandwich.

You had water in your shoes.

They had tickets to the show.

When used with another verb, **have**, **has**, and **had** are **helping verbs**.

Felipe **has read** for three hours.

I **had purchased** new sunglasses.

We **have hiked** up that hill.

Put **have**, **has**, or **had** before the subject when asking a question.

Have you **opened** the trunk?

Has Jim **entered** the office?

Had he **repaired** the refrigerator?

4.14 The Verb Do

Do is an irregular verb that can be used as a **main verb**. **Do** and its forms **does** and **did** can also be used as helping verbs.

When used alone, **do**, **does**, or **did** is the main verb in the sentence. **Do** and **does** are the present tense forms of the verb.

If the subject is **I**, **you**, **we**, **they**, or is **plural**, use the verb **do**.

They do the yard work.

We do the dishes.

The **runners do** their best.

If the subject is **he**, **she**, **it**, or is **singular**, use **does**.

She does a lot of reading.

Lou does the housework.

The **hawk does** its hunting in the morning.

Did is the **past tense** form of the verb **do** and can be used with **singular** or **plural** subjects.

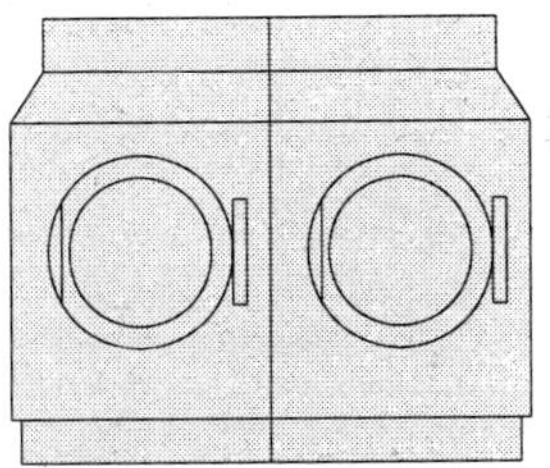

You did the laundry.

Sam did an amazing job!

The **baby did** something new.

When used with another verb, **do**, **does**, and **did** are **helping verbs**.

The doctor **did examine** my hand.

The children **do enjoy** their new swing set.

Shelby **does practice** every day.

Put **do**, **does**, or **did** before the subject when asking a question.

Did she **return** your book?

Do you **play** on a soccer team?

Does Michael **know** the answer?

4.15 Writing a Narrative Paragraph

A **narrative paragraph** usually tells a story and is often used to describe what a person does over a period of time. It usually narrates an event that happened to the writer.

A narrative paragraph must contain a topic sentence, detail sentences, and time order. Remember, some time order words that can be used are **first**, **second**, **third**, **next**, **last**, **before**, **then**, **finally**, and **after**.

When writing a paragraph, you must first plan what you are going to write. Think of a topic and then make a list of ideas about the topic.

Example:

Topic→ our trip to Grandpa's house

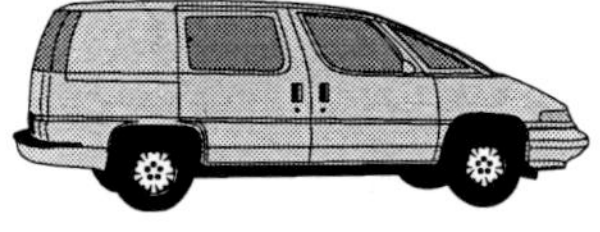

Ideas:
waking up early
Dad gets food
singing and playing games
spending time with Grandpa

Think of the order in which you will write the details. Make sure that the order makes sense. Also, make sure that all the details are related to the topic.

Think of a topic sentence that tells the main idea of the paragraph, and then you can write the paragraph describing the event. The **first person** pronouns **I**, **me**, **my**, **mine**, **we**, **us**, **our**, and **ours** are often used since narrative paragraphs are usually told in the first person.

Example:

A Trip to Grandpa's House

Going to Grandpa's house is always a fun day for my family. First we have to wake up early because we have a three-hour drive to his house. We love the food Dad buys for us to eat while we are on the road. After we eat, we sing and play games in the car. Finally, we arrive at Grandpa's house and spend the day with him. Then we leave to go home, and the whole trip starts over again.

This paragraph tells a story about a fun trip to Grandpa's house. It has a title and also a topic sentence that tells what the paragraph will be about. The detail sentences give information about why the trip is fun. The time order words **first**, **after**, **finally**, and **then** are used to help give order to the paragraph.

Finally, you should edit your paragraph. Make sure you indented the first sentence, you started all of your sentences with a capital letter, you ended each sentence with the correct punctuation, and you spelled each word correctly.

Chapter 4 Review

Action Verbs: **Action verbs** are words that tell what action the subject of a sentence is doing.

Direct Objects: The noun or pronoun that receives the direct action of the verb is called the **direct object**. The verb used with a direct object is always an action verb. To identify the direct object, say the subject and verb followed by **what** or **whom**.

On a sentence diagram, the direct object is placed on the same line with the subject and predicate. It is separated from the predicate by a short vertical line that does not break through the horizontal line.

Alyson hugged **Bradyn**.

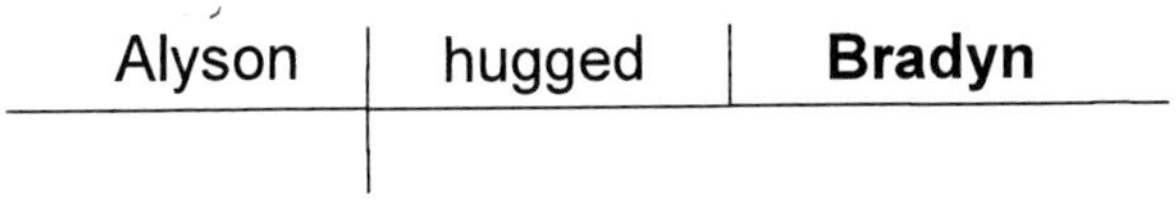

Alyson	hugged	**Bradyn**

Not every sentence has a direct object. If nothing answers the question **what** or **whom**, then there is **no** direct object.

Linking Verbs: **Linking verbs** are words that do not show action or tell what the subject is doing. They link the subject to a word in the predicate that names or describes it.

<u>Predicate Nouns</u>: A **predicate noun** is a word that follows a linking verb and renames the subject of the sentence.

On a diagram, the predicate noun is placed on the same line with the subject and predicate. It is separated from the predicate by a short diagonal line that does not break through the horizontal line.

Lisa is my **cousin**.

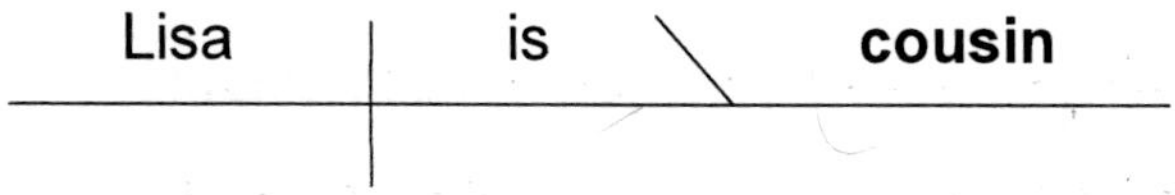

Lisa | is \ **cousin**

<u>Contractions</u>: A **contraction** is a word made by combining two other words. When the words are combined, some letters are dropped and are replaced by an **apostrophe (')**.

<u>Helping Verbs</u>: **Helping verbs** help another verb and are sometimes called **auxiliary verbs**. They come before the main verb to tell about the action.

<u>Verb Phrases</u>: A **verb phrase** contains a main verb plus one or more helping verbs. The main verb is the last word in the verb phrase.

<u>**Verb Tenses**</u>: **Tense** tells when the action occurred or will occur.

Verbs that show what is happening now are said to be in the **present tense**.

If the subject means **it**, **she**, or **he**, then add **-s** to the verb to show present tense. Do not use an **-s** with subjects that are **I**, **you**, or are **plural**. Some verbs end with a **consonant letter** followed by a **y**. Change the **y** to **i** and add **-es**.

Verbs that tell about something happening in the future are called **future tense**. The future tense is formed by using **will** or **shall** before the verb.

Verbs that tell what has already happened are called **past tense**.

To form the past tense of most verbs, add **-ed** to the verb. For some verbs that end with **e**, drop the **e** and add **-ed**. Some verbs end with a **consonant letter** and a **y**. Change the **y** to **i** and add **-ed**. Some verbs end with a **single vowel** followed by a **single consonant**. **Double the final consonant** and add -**ed**.

The **progressive verb tense** shows if the **action is happening**, **was happening**, or **will be happening**.

The **present progressive tense verb** is formed by combining **am**, **is**, or **are** with the **-ing** form of a **verb**.

The **past progressive tense verb** is formed by combining **was** or **were** with the **-ing** form of a **verb**.

The **future progressive tense verb** is formed by combining **will be** with the -**ing** form of a **verb**.

Irregular Verbs: An **irregular verb** is one that does not form its past tense by adding **-ed**. Instead, the spelling of these verbs is changed.

For some irregular verbs, the past tense without a helping verb is the same as the past tense with a helping verb. Other irregular verbs have different past forms. One is used without a helping verb and the other is used with the helping verbs **has**, **have**, or **had**.

Subject – Verb Agreement: In a sentence, the verb must agree with the subject in order to make sense. A singular subject must have a singular verb, and a plural subject must have a plural verb.

If the subject of the sentence is **singular** or the pronoun **he**, **she**, or **it**, then add an -**s** to the verb. This is called the -**s form** of the verb. Verbs in the present tense frequently end with -**s**.

If the subject of the sentence is **plural** or the pronoun **I**, **you**, **we**, or **they**, then do not add -**s** to the verb. This is called the **plain form** of the verb.

<u>The Verb Have</u>: **Have** is an irregular verb that shows that somebody owns something. When used alone, **have**, **has**, or **had** is the **main verb** in the sentence.
-If the subject is **I**, **you**, **we**, **they**, or is **plural**, use **have.**
-If the subject is **he**, **she**, **it**, or is **singular**, use **has**.

Had is the **past tense** form of the verb **have** and can be used with **singular** or **plural** subjects.

When used with another verb, **have**, **has**, and **had** are **helping verbs**. Put **have**, **has**, or **had** before the subject when asking a question.

<u>The Verb Do</u>: **Do** is an irregular verb. When used alone, **do**, **does**, or **did** is the **main verb** in the sentence.

-If the subject is **I**, **you**, **we**, **they**, or is **plural**, use the verb **do**.
-If the subject is **he**, **she**, **it**, or is **singular**, use **does**.

Did is the **past tense** form of the verb **do** and can be used with **singular** or **plural** subjects.

When used with another verb, **do**, **does**, and **did** are **helping verbs**.

Put **do**, **does**, or **did** before the subject when asking a question.

Chapter 5

Growing with Adjectives

5.1 Adjectives

An **adjective** is a word that describes a **noun** or pronoun and may answer the question **what kind**, **how many**, **which one**, or **whose**. An adjective usually comes before the noun or the pronoun that it describes.

Some adjectives answer the question **what kind** and tell how things look, smell, sound, feel, or taste.

The **white** cat purred.

We ate **delicious** cookies.

We have a **new** car.

The **old** engine makes **black** smoke.

Some adjectives answer the question **how many**. Number words such as **one**, **two**, and **three**, and words like **several**, **some**, **numerous**, **all**, **no**, **many**, and **much** are adjectives that tell how many.

Seven apples fell.

I have **four** sisters.

Many people arrived at the park.

I picked **some** flowers.

Some adjectives answer the question **which one**. The words **this**, **that**, **these**, and **those** and words such as **first**, **second**, and **third** tell **which one**.

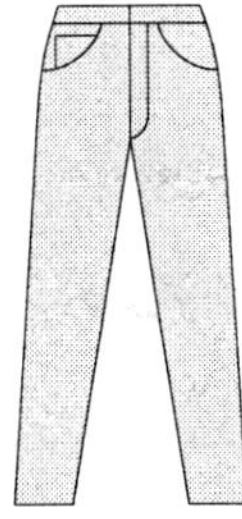

I like **these** pants.

This glass is broken.

I am in **fourth** grade.

Tomorrow is Ted's **ninth** birthday.

Some adjectives answer the question **whose**. Possessive nouns like **Jill's**, **snake's**, and **man's**, and possessive pronouns like **my**, **our**, **your**, **their**, **her**, **his**, and **its** are used as adjectives to tell **whose**.

Annie's brother runs fast.

The **bird's** nest fell.

My dad made **our** dinner.

Who made **your** scarf?

Adjective Order

When more than one **adjective** is used to describe a **noun**, all the adjectives need to be placed in the **proper order**.

Example:

The company makes ***pretty green farming*** equipment.

Adjectives like **pretty** and **green** are **opinion adjectives**. They tell what someone **thinks** about someone or something. **Opinion** adjectives usually appear before **fact** adjectives.

Example:

A ***large young red*** cardinal flew past our window.

Adjectives like **large**, **young**, and **red** are **fact adjectives** that give us factual information about the **size**, **age**, **shape**, **color**, **origin**, **material**, and **purpose**, of someone or something.

When you use more than one **fact adjective**, you put them in this order, after **opinion adjectives**:

OPINION	SIZE	AGE	SHAPE	COLOR	ORIGIN	MATERIAL	PURPOSE
delicious	large	old	round	blue	French	metal	drawing
beautiful	tiny	young	dented	violet	northern	paper	cutting

Examples:

Sherry is wearing a **beautiful yellow** dress.

We live in an **old brick** house.

↑ ↑

age material

He sits behind a **large square drawing** desk.

Dad drives a **new white German** car.

I bought **beautiful pink** flowers.

↑ ↑

opinion color

Articles

The words **a**, **an**, and **the** are articles, which are a type of adjective, that tell that a noun is coming. They are also called **noun markers.**

a picture **an** elephant **the** boy

The article **a** is used when a word begins with a consonant sound.

a letter

a spider

a dollar

The article **an** is used when a word begins with a vowel sound.

an owl

an animal

an error

The article **the** is used when talking about a particular person or thing.

the girl

the mountains

the Kentucky Derby

5.2 Diagramming Adjectives

On a sentence diagram, the **adjective** is placed on a slanted line under the subject, direct object, or predicate noun it describes.

The **white** cat purred.

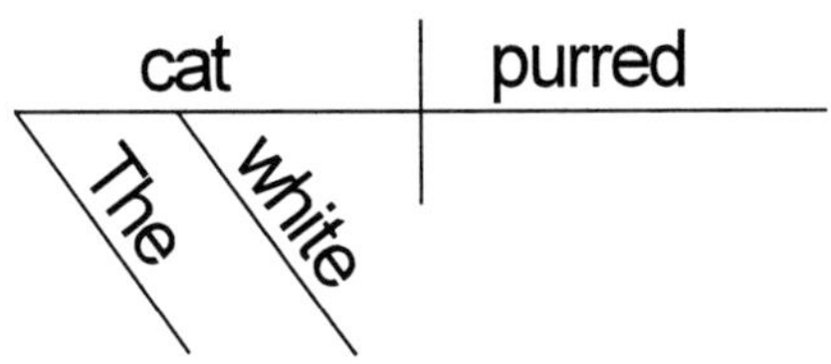

Remember, the articles **a**, **an**, and **the** are adjectives and are also placed on a slanted line under the corresponding noun or pronoun.

More examples:

The apples fell.

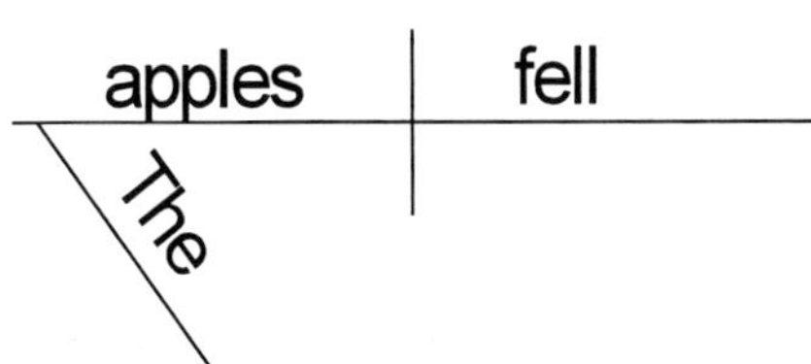

I like **these** pants.

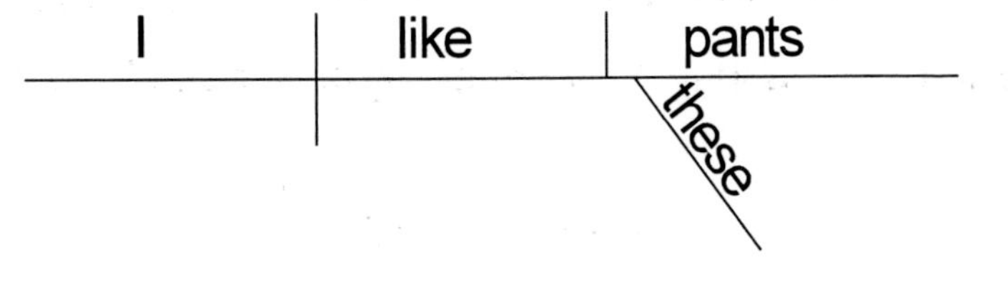

My dad is **a great** chef.

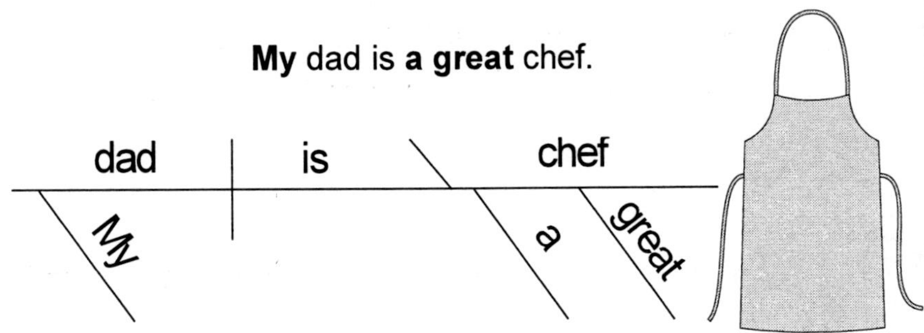

The old engine makes **black** smoke.

engine | makes | smoke

The old black

5.3 This, That, These, and Those

When the words **this**, **that**, **these**, and **those** are followed by nouns, they are being used as **adjectives**.

That bike is mine.

In this sentence, the word **that** is an **adjective** describing the noun **bike**. It is telling **which one**.

When the words **this**, **that**, **these**, and **those** are not followed by a noun, they are **pronouns**.

That is mine.

In this sentence, the word **that** is a **pronoun** and has taken the place of the noun.

This and **that** are used with **singular** nouns.

(adjective) **This** rope is long. *(pronoun)* **This** is long.

(adjective) **That** rope is short. *(pronoun)* **That** is short.

These and **those** are used with **plural** nouns.

(adjective) **These** rolls are hot. *(pronoun)* **These** are hot.

(adjective) **Those** rolls are cold. *(pronoun)* **Those** are cold.

This and **these** are used to tell about nouns that express **nearness**.

(adjective) **This** car is fast. *(pronoun)* **This** is fast.

(adjective) **These** cars are slow. *(pronoun)* **These** are slow.

That and **those** are used to tell about nouns that express **distance**.

(adjective) **That** light is on. *(pronoun)* **That** is on.

(adjective) **Those** lights are off. *(pronoun)* **Those** are off.

Never use **this**, **that**, **these**, or **those** with the word **here** or **there**.

Incorrect: That there book is small.

Correct: That book is small.

Incorrect: These here shoes are tight.

Correct: These shoes are tight.

5.4 Proper Adjectives

A **proper adjective** is a word made from a proper noun. Proper adjectives always begin with a capital letter.

We are studying **Roman** sculptures.

Daniel waved the **Australian** flag.

In the first sentence, the proper adjective **Roman** is formed from the proper noun **Rome** and describes the noun **sculptures.** In the second sentence, the proper adjective **Australian** is formed from the proper noun **Australia** and describes the noun **flag**.

More examples:

Proper Noun	Proper Adjective
Mexico	**Mexican** food
Africa	**African** violets
France	**French** bread
Italy	**Italian** sausage
Japan	**Japanese** language
Shakespeare	**Shakespearean** play

Some **proper adjectives** are just proper nouns used as adjectives. The spelling does not change.

Proper Noun	Proper Adjective
New York	**New York** pizza
Arctic	**Arctic** storm
United States	**United States** citizen
Paris	**Paris** fashions
January	**January** snow
Thanksgiving	**Thanksgiving** dinner

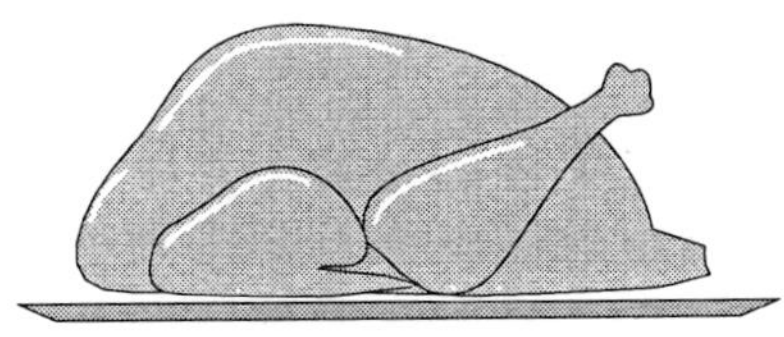

5.5 Adjectives that Compare

Many **adjectives** are used to compare people or things. There are three degrees of comparison: **positive** (the simple quality), **comparative** (with one of two objects), and **superlative** (with one of more than two objects).

The endings **-er** or **-est** are added to show comparison with adjectives that have one or two syllables.

More and **most** are often used with adjectives that have three or more syllables and some two-syllable adjectives.

Usually, in the comparative degree, when comparing **two** people or things, the ending **-er** is added to most adjectives.

Jeffrey is **older** than Tony.

Today is **hotter** than yesterday.

Some adjectives with two or more syllables use the word **more**.

Chad was **more excited** than his brother.

That coat is **more expensive** than this one.

When comparing **three** or **more** people or things, in the superlative degree, the ending **-est** is typically used.

Paloma is the **shortest** person I know.

My brother was the **fastest** player on the team.

Some adjectives with two or more syllables use the word **most** to compare.

This is the **most comfortable** chair.

Aunt Libby is the **most patient** person I know.

Do not add **-er** to an adjective at the same time you use **more**.

Incorrect: This test was more easier than the last test.

Correct: This test was **easier** than the last test.

Incorrect: Will is more generouser than Luke.

Correct: Will is **more generous** than Luke.

Also, do not add **-est** to an adjective at the same time you use **most**.

Incorrect: I think daisies are the most prettiest flowers.

Correct: I think daisies are the **prettiest** flowers.

Incorrect: He is the most carefullest boy I know.

Correct: He is the **most careful** boy I know.

5.6 Forming Adjectives that Compare

For most short adjectives with one syllable (and sometimes two syllables), simply add **-er** or **-est** to the word.

Positive	Comparative	Superlative
fast	fast**er**	fast**est**
weak	weak**er**	weak**est**
new	new**er**	new**est**
sharp	sharp**er**	sharp**est**
small	small**er**	small**est**

Some adjectives need spelling changes before you can add **-er** or **-est.**

For some short adjectives that end with an **e,** drop the **e** and add **-er** or **-est**.

Positive	Comparative	Superlative
nice	nic**er**	nic**est**
rare	rar**er**	rar**est**
wide	wid**er**	wid**est**
late	lat**er**	lat**est**
close	clos**er**	clos**est**

For some one- or two-syllable adjectives that end with a **consonant** and **y**, change the **y** to **i**, then add **-er** or **-est**.

Positive	Comparative	Superlative
noisy	nois**ier**	nois**iest**
silly	sill**ier**	sill**iest**
muddy	mudd**ier**	mudd**iest**
happy	happ**ier**	happ**iest**
heavy	heav**ier**	heav**iest**

For some adjectives that end with a single consonant after a short vowel, double the final consonant and add **-er** or **-est**.

Positive	Comparative	Superlative
dim	dim**mer**	dim**mest**
sad	sad**der**	sad**dest**
wet	wet**ter**	wet**test**
big	big**ger**	big**gest**
thin	thin**ner**	thin**nest**

Some **adjectives** that are used to compare are **irregular**. These change form when they are used to compare.

Positive	Comparative	Superlative
good	better	best
bad	worse	worst
many	more	most
much	more	most
little	less	least

Better, **worse**, **more**, and **less** are used to compare two nouns.

This pineapple is **better** than that pineapple.

Today's weather is **worse** than yesterday's.

Paige has read **more** books than Philip.

Marius ate **less** food than Isaac.

Best, **worst**, **most**, and **least** are used to compare three or more nouns.

Chuck is the **best** hitter on the team.

This is the **worst** snow storm we have ever had.

James is having the **most** fun ever.

I had the **least** pizza of all.

Do not add **-er** or **-est** to the adjectives **good**, **bad**, **many**, **much**, and **little.**

Incorrect: Joel had the littlest homeruns of anyone.

Correct: Joel had the **least** amount of homeruns of all.

Incorrect: I had mucher fun than you.

Correct: I had **more** fun than you.

Also, do not use **more** and **most** with the comparing forms of these adjectives.

Incorrect: This book was more good than that book.

Correct: This book was **better** than that book.

Incorrect: We had the most bad of all.

Correct: We had the **worst** time of all.

5.7 Adjective Suffixes

A **suffix** is a word part added to the **end** of a base word to make a new word. Suffixes usually change the meaning of the word.

Certain suffixes can change some words into adjectives. A few adjective suffixes are **-able**, **-ful**, and **-less**.

The suffix **-able** means **can** or **able to.**

bend + able = bend**able**

enjoy + able = enjoy**able**

The suffix **-able** at the end of the word **bend** means **able to bend**. The suffix **-able** at the end of the word **enjoy** means **can enjoy**.

More examples:

wash**able** = able to wash		mov**able** = can move	
accept**able** = able to accept		lov**able** = can love	

The suffix **-ful** means **full of**. Notice that it has only one "l" instead of two as in full.

help + ful = help**ful**

wonder + ful = wonder**ful**

The suffix **-ful** at the end of the word **help** means **full of help**. The suffix **-ful** at the end of **wonder** means **full of wonder**.

More examples:

grace**ful** = full of grace   pain**ful** = full of pain

skill**ful** = full of skill   thank**ful** = full of thanks

The suffix **-less** means **without**.

fear + less = fear**less**

hope + less = hope**less**

The suffix **-less** at the end of the word **fear** means **without fear**. The suffix **-less** at the end of **hope** means **without hope**.

More examples:

care**less** = without care   end**less** = without end

taste**less** = without taste   seed**less** = without seeds

5.8 Building Sentences with Adjectives

Adjectives add details to sentences and make them more interesting. Adding detail can also make things seem real.

 Brother saw snakes. 

My little brother saw **two red** snakes.

The first sentence is short and does not give much detail. The second sentence gives more information about Brother and the snakes and makes the sentence more interesting. Adjectives were used to tell **whose** and **which** brother. Adjectives were also used to tell **how many** and **what kind** of snakes.

More examples:

Without Adjectives: Children make crafts.

With Adjectives: **Three happy** children make **colorful** crafts.

Without Adjectives: Puppy chews shoes.

With Adjectives: **That brown** puppy chews **Joe's two** shoes.

Without Adjectives: Family eats food.

With Adjectives: **My large** family eats **some delicious** food.

Without Adjectives: Aunt Lyn lives in the house.

With Adjectives: **Her** Aunt Lyn lives in the **third white** house.

5.9 Writing Friendly Letters and Postcards

A **friendly letter** is a personal letter or social note that is usually written to a friend and often contains information about you. It may also ask questions about the friend to whom you are writing. There are five parts to a friendly letter.

The **first** part is the **heading**. The heading is in the upper right hand corner of the letter and contains your address with the date on the last line.

The **second** part is the **greeting**. The greeting usually begins with the word **Dear** followed by the person's name. Be sure to place a comma after the name.

Dear Mrs. Rodriguez,

Dear Aunt Susan,

The **third** part is the **body** of the letter. This part contains the message you want to write, including all of the information and questions for the person to whom you are writing. Each paragraph should be indented.

The **fourth** part is the **closing**. Always capitalize the first word and place a comma after the closing.

Your friend**,**

Sincerely**,**

The **fifth** part is your name or **signature** after the closing.

Example of a friendly letter:

Heading → 472 Red Street
Houston, TX 77008
March 19, 20-

Greeting → Dear Aunt Susan,

Body → Mom said that I will be able to stay with you this summer. I will stay for two weeks in the month of June.

I am excited to spend time with you, Uncle George, and my cousins. Will we be able to visit the zoo?

Closing → Your nephew,

Signature → Eric

A **postcard** is something people send to friends or family when they are away from home, usually on vacation. It is typically a quick note letting the person know you are having a good time and that you are thinking of him or her.

Example:

Postage stamp→

Postcard

Greeting → Dear Jerry,

Body → We are having fun on our trip. I can't wait to tell you all about it. See you soon!

Closing → Your friend,

Signature → Michael

Address → Jerry Smith
123 Main St.
Miami FL 33178

5.10 Writing Business Letters

Another common type of letter is a **business letter**. A business letter is more formal than a friendly letter and is written when a person wants to request information, order a product, let someone know about a problem, or share an opinion.

A business letter has the same five parts that a friendly letter has, plus one additional part, the **inside address**. The six parts include the **heading**, **inside address**, **greeting**, **body**, **closing**, and **signature**.

The **heading** is in the upper right hand corner of the letter and contains your address with the date on the last line.

The **inside address** has the name and title of the person or company who will receive the letter. It also includes the address of the person to whom the letter is being sent.

The **greeting** usually starts with the word **Dear** followed by the person's name. However, if you do not know the name of the person to whom you are writing, you can write Dear Sir or Dear Madam. Also, use a colon (:) after the greeting rather than a comma, as you would in a friendly letter.

Dear Mr. Jones:

Dear Madam:

The **body** is the main part of the business letter and is where you explain why you are writing. This part should be short and to the point and should tell what the problem is or explain what you are requesting.

The **closing** is the ending to the letter. Always capitalize the first word and place a comma after the closing.

Best regards,

Sincerely,

The **signature** is your name after the closing including your first and last names.

Example of a business letter:

Heading → 472 Red Street
Houston, TX 77008
March 19, 20-

Inside address → Mr. John Smith
New York City Tourism Office
123 Tourism Street
New York, NY 10003

Greeting → Dear Mr. Smith:

Body → My family and I will be vacationing in New York City this September. I would appreciate any information that you could send me about the local museums and parks.

Closing → Thank you,

Signature → Eric Cortez

5.11 Other Types of Social Notes

There are other types of personal and social notes. Two are **invitations** and **thank you letters**.

An **invitation** should answer the five questions **what**, **when**, **who**, **why**, and **where**.

What type of event is being held? Is it a party, a picnic, or a barbecue? **When** is the event taking place? Provide the date and time. **Who** is the party for? **Why** is the party being given? Is it for a birthday, an anniversary, or a graduation? **Where** is the party taking place? Provide the address and directions.

Often, an invitation will ask that the person let it be known if he or she will be attending the event. If you need to know how many people will be at the party and who is attending, be sure to include a telephone number on the invitation. This is called the **RSVP** which means "**please respond**."

Example:	**What**:	Surprise party!
	When:	April 12, 20-- at 2:00 p.m.
	Who:	For Jada Conway
	Why:	Her 9th birthday
	Where:	Potter's Restaurant
	R.S.V.P.	555-20xx

Thank you letters are written to show gratitude for something that someone has done for you or given to you. A thank you letter should be written as soon as possible after the thoughtful act. Be sure to mention the gift or occasion in the letter.

Example:

Dear Aunt Justine,

The art supplies are terrific. You always know just what I want. Thank you so much for such a great present.

Love,

Carol

5.12 Addressing an Envelope

After you have finished writing your friendly letter, business letter, invitation, or thank you letter, you can place it in an **envelope**, add a stamp, and send it through the mail. However, before the letter is mailed, you will need to put the correct information on the envelope.

Write your name and address in the upper left hand corner of the envelope. This is called the **return address** and tells who is sending the letter.

In the center of the envelope, write the name and address of the person to whom the letter is being sent. This is called the **mailing address**.

Finally, put a **stamp** in the upper right hand corner and place it in the mailbox.

Carol Clark
555 Robin Hood Lane
Albany NY 12204

stamp

Justine Clark
123 Main Street
Wichita KS 67203

Chapter 5 Review

Adjectives: An **adjective** is a word that describes a **noun** or **pronoun** and may answer the question **what kind**, **how many**, **which one**, or **whose**. An adjective usually comes before the noun or the pronoun that it describes. When more than one **adjective** is used to describe a **noun**, all the adjectives need to be placed in the **proper order**. **Opinion** adjectives usually appear before **fact** adjectives.

On a sentence diagram, the **adjective** is placed on a slanted line under the subject, direct object, or predicate noun it describes.

The old engine makes **black** smoke.

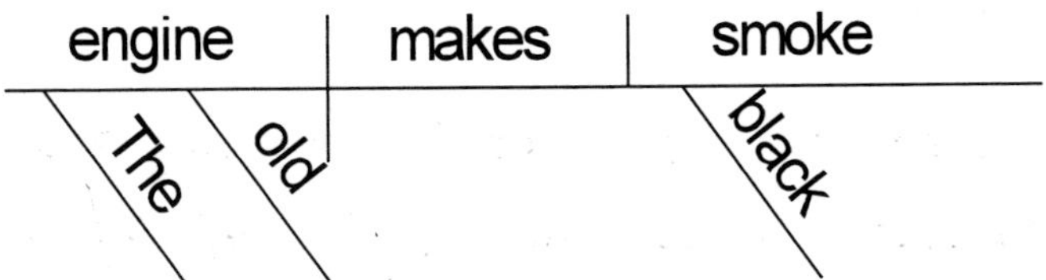

This, That, These, and Those: When the words **this**, **that**, **these**, and **those** are followed by nouns, they are being used as **adjectives**. When the words **this**, **that**,

these, and **those** are not followed by a noun, they are **pronouns**.

-**This** and **that** are used with **singular** nouns.

-**These** and **those** are used with **plural** nouns.

-**This** and **these** are used to tell about nouns that express **nearness**.

-**That** and **those** are used to tell about nouns that express **distance**.

Proper Adjectives: A **proper adjective** is a word made from a proper noun. Proper adjectives always begin with a capital letter. Some proper adjectives are just proper nouns used as adjectives, and the spelling does not change.

Adjectives that Compare: Many **adjectives** are used to compare nouns.

-Usually, when comparing **two** nouns, the ending **-er** is added to most adjectives. Some adjectives with two or more syllables use the word **more**.

-When comparing **three** or **more** nouns, the ending -**est** is typically used. Some adjectives with two or more syllables use the word **most** to compare.

-Do not add **-er** to an adjective at the same time you use **more**. Also, do not add **-est** to an adjective at the same time you use **most**.

<u>Forming Adjectives that Compare</u>:

-For most short adjectives with one syllable (and sometimes two syllables), simply add **-er** or **-est** to the word.
-For some short adjectives that end with an **e,** drop the **e** and add **-er** or **-est**.
-For some one- or two-syllable adjectives that end with a **consonant** and **y**, change the **y** to **i**, then add **-er** or **-est**.
-For some adjectives that end with a single consonant after a short vowel, double the final consonant and add **-er** or **-est**.

Some adjectives that are used to compare are irregular.

-Better, **worse**, **more**, and **less** are used to compare two nouns.
-Best, **worst**, **most**, and **least** are used to compare three or more nouns.
-Do not add **-er** or **-est** to the adjectives **good**, **bad**, **many**, **much**, and **little.** Also, do not use **more** and **most** with the comparing forms of these adjectives.

Adjective Suffixes: A few suffixes change some words into adjectives.

-The suffix **-able** means **can** or **able to.**

-The suffix **-ful** means **full of**.

-The suffix **-less** means **without**.

Using Adjectives: Adjectives add details to sentences, make them more interesting, and make things seem real.

Chapter 6

Growing with Adverbs

6.1 Adverbs

An **adverb** is a word that tells more about a **verb.** Adverbs tell **when**, **where**, or **how** something is done. An adverb works with a verb to make its meaning more clear. Adverbs often end in **-ly**.

Adverbs can tell **when** about the verb. Some adverbs that tell when are **late**, **later**, **now**, **soon**, **today**, **tomorrow**, **yesterday**, **whenever**, **always**, **never**, **sometimes**, **first**, **forever**, **daily**, **then**, and **afterward**.

We sang **today.**

Andrea drew a picture **earlier.**

Leandro **never** eats chocolate.

Jana **always** changes her mind.

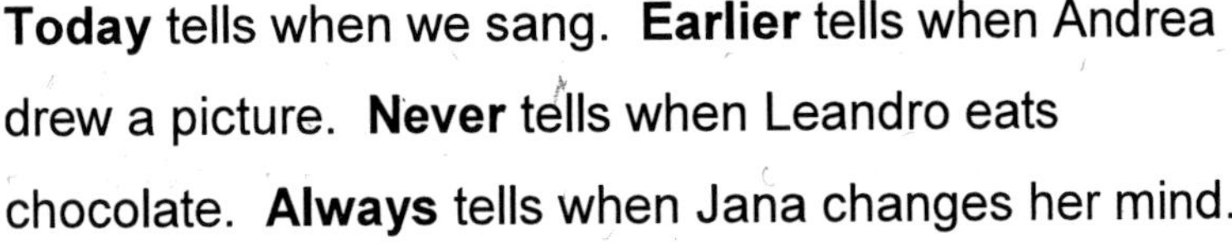

Today tells when we sang. **Earlier** tells when Andrea drew a picture. **Never** tells when Leandro eats chocolate. **Always** tells when Jana changes her mind.

Adverbs can tell **where** about the verb. Some adverbs that tell where are **here**, **away**, **forward**, **near**, **far**, **there**, **nowhere**, **everywhere**, **somewhere**, **anywhere**, **in**, **inside**, **out**, **outside**, **up**, **upstairs**, **down**, **downstairs**, and **around**.

Bill rushed **outside**.

Juan fell **forward**.

The children went **there**.

Karen sat **down**.

Outside tells where Bill rushed. **Forward** tells where Juan fell. **There** tells where the children went. **Down** tells where Karen sat.

Adverbs can tell **how** about the verb. Some adverbs that tell how are **bravely**, **fast**, **neatly**, **quietly**, **eagerly**.

More examples:

Peter worked **carefully**.

He stopped **suddenly**.

She yelled **loudly.**

They ran **quickly.**

Carefully tells how Peter worked. **Suddenly** tells how he stopped. **Loudly** tells how she yelled. **Quickly** tells how they ran.

The words **when**, **where**, and **how** are also adverbs.

When did Arturo leave?

Where is Maria going?

How did you sleep?

Adjectives can often be changed into adverbs by adding **-ly**.

Shamar is a **quiet** boy.

He sits **quietly**.

In the first sentence, **quiet** is an adjective describing the noun **boy**. When the **-ly** is added, the word becomes an adverb. In the second sentence, **quietly** is an adverb describing the verb **sits**. It tells **how** he sits.

More examples:

careful → careful**ly**

sudden → sudden**ly**

patient → patient**ly**

swift → swift**ly**

bright → bright**ly**

quiet → quiet**ly**

6.2 Diagramming Adverbs

On a sentence diagram, the **adverb** is placed on a slanted line under the verb it describes.

We sang **today**.

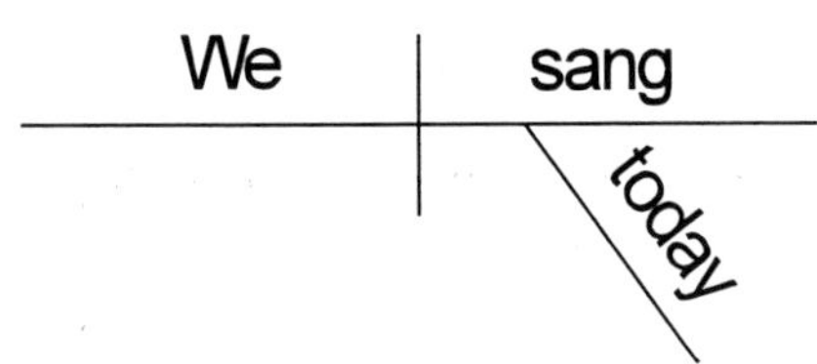

More examples:

Bill rushed **outside**.

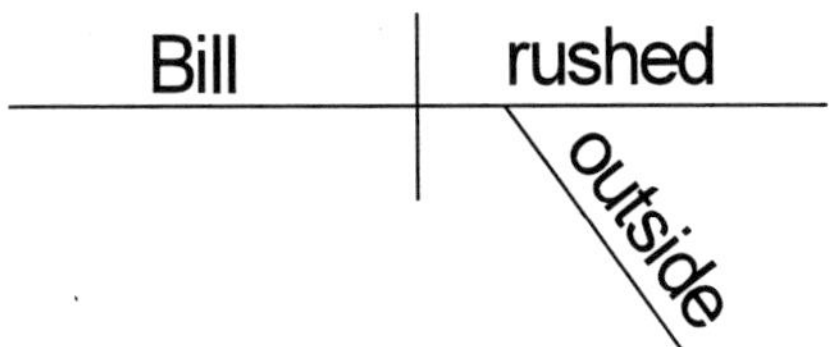

He stopped **suddenly**.

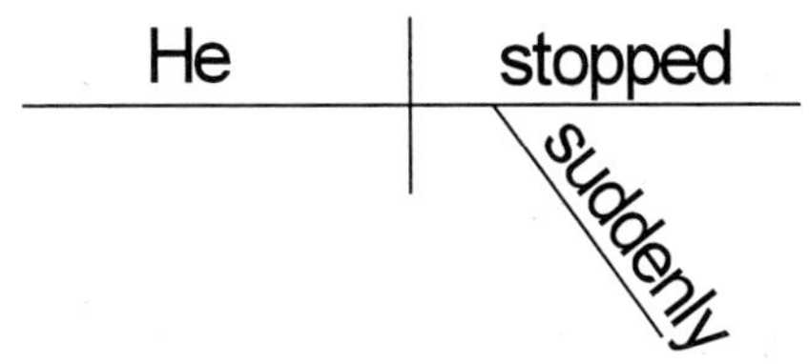

When did Arturo leave?

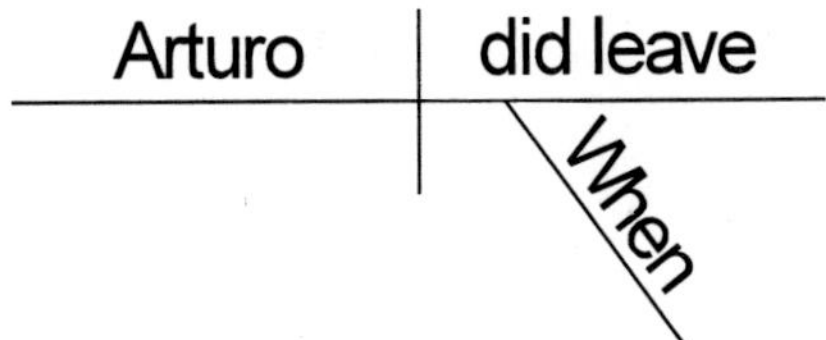

Where is Maria going?

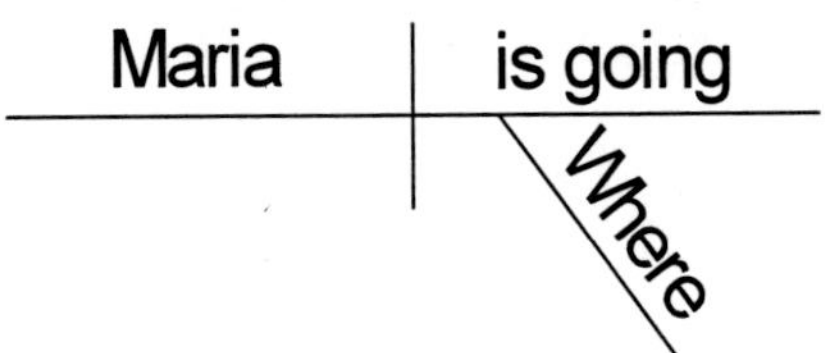

How did you sleep?

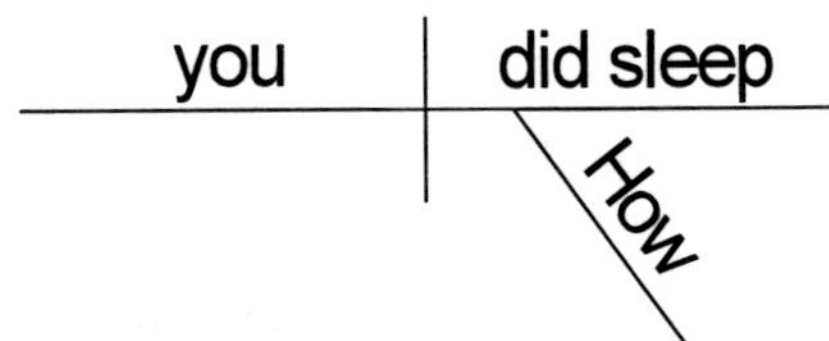

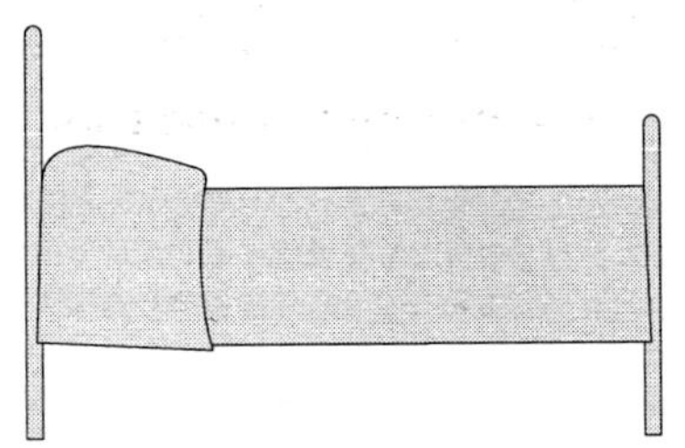

6.3 Adverb Placement

In a sentence, an **adverb** can come before or after the verb. Sometimes it can be in different locations in the sentence.

Adverbs can be found at the **beginning** of a sentence.

Suddenly he stopped.
Quietly Anna closed the door.
Yesterday we went to the zoo.
Usually he sits by us.

Adverbs can be found in the **middle** of a sentence.

Jamie **always** jogs.
I **never** play in the snow.
The dog barked **loudly** at the children.
She **slowly** left the room.

Also, adverbs can be found at the **end** of a sentence.

We are leaving **today**.

Dad went **outside**.

Jack waits **patiently**.

The day passed **quickly**.

Even though an adverb can be located in different positions in a sentence, it is still placed on a diagram under the verb it describes.

Suddenly he stopped.

He **suddenly** stopped.

He stopped **suddenly**.

These sentences are all diagrammed in the same way.

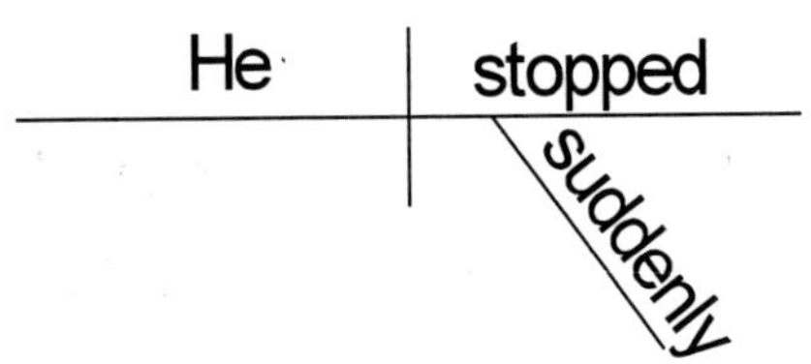

6.4 Adverbs that Compare

Many **adverbs** can be used to compare actions. As with adjectives, with adverbs there are three degrees of comparison: **positive** (the simple quality), **comparative** (with one of two objects), and **superlative** (with one of more than two objects).

The endings **-er** or **-est** are added to show comparison with most one-syllable adverbs. **More** and **most** are often used with most adverbs of two or more syllables.

When comparing **two** actions, in the comparative degree, the ending **-er** is added to most one-syllable adverbs. Add the word **more** before most adverbs of two or more syllables.

Adam runs **faster** than Sandy.

Xavier sleds **more carefully** than his sister.

In the first sentence, we are comparing the actions of **Adam** and **Sandy**. The adverb **faster** describes how Adam runs compared to Sandy. In the second sentence, we are comparing the actions of **Xavier** and his **sister**. **More carefully** describes how Xavier sleds compared to his sister.

When comparing **three** or **more** actions, in the superlative degree, the ending **-est** is typically used with most one-syllable adverbs. Add the word **most** before most adverbs of two or more syllables.

Amy tries **hardest** of the entire team.

Brett waits **most patiently** of all the boys.

In the first sentence, we are comparing the actions of **Amy** and **the entire team**. The adverb **hardest** describes how Amy tries compared to the team. In the second sentence, we are comparing the actions of **Brett** and **all the boys**. **Most patiently** describes how Brett waits compared to the boys.

More examples:

Positive	Comparative	Superlative
fast	faster	fastest
late	later	latest
high	higher	highest
loudly	more loudly	most loudly
softly	more softly	most softly

Some adverbs are irregular and change their spelling when used to compare.

Positive	Comparative	Superlative
well	better	best
badly	worse	worst
far	farther	farthest
little	less	least

Do not add **-er** to an adverb at the same time you use **more**.

Incorrect: Sam arrived more later than I did.

Correct: Sam arrived **later** than I did.

Also, do not add **-est** to an adverb at the same time you use **most**.

Incorrect: A cheetah runs most swiftliest of all cats.

Correct: A cheetah runs **most swiftly** of all cats.

Also, don't use **-est** or **most** when comparing two actions.

Incorrect: Of the two, William whistled most loud.

Incorrect: Of the two, William whistled loudest.

Correct: Of the two, William whistled **louder**.

6.5 Relative Pronouns and Relative Adverbs

A **relative pronoun** introduces a group of words, or a clause, that tells more about a **noun**. Words that often act as **relative pronouns** are **who**, **whose**, **which**, and **that**.

Use the relative pronouns **who** and **whose** when referring to people.

He is the *boy* **who** won the race.

(**who won the race** tells more about the noun **boy**)

The *woman* **whose** dog is barking is Mrs. James.

(**whose dog is barking** tells more about the noun **woman**)

Use the relative pronouns **which** and **that** when referring to animals and things.

That is the *book* **which** Joe lent to me.

(**which Joe lent to me** tells more about the noun **book**)

This is the *puppy* **that** my cousin adopted.

(**that my cousin adopted** tells more about the noun **puppy**)

The pronouns **who**, **which**, and **whose** can be **interrogative pronouns** (asking a question) or **relative pronouns** depending on how they are used in a sentence.

Interrogative: **Who** said that?
Relative: I know **who** said that.

Interrogative: **Whose** keys are on the table?
Relative: The man **whose** keys are on the table is John.

Like a relative pronoun, a **relative adverb** also introduces a group of words, or a clause, that tells more about a **noun**. Words that often act as **relative adverbs** are **where**, **when**, and **why**.

The *house* **where** we live is very large.
(**where we live** tells more about the noun **house**)

June is the *month* **when** we go on vacation.
(**when we go on vacation** tells more about the noun **month**)

Do you know the *reason* **why** he left?
(**why he left** tells more about the noun **reason**)

6.6 Double Negatives

A word that means **no** or **not** is called a **negative word**. The words **no**, **not**, **none**, **nothing**, **nowhere**, **neither**, **nobody**, **no one**, and **never** are common negative words. If you use any of these negative words in your sentences, your statements will be negative.

We travel.

We **never** travel.

Notice that by adding the negative word **never**, the sentence becomes negative.

The use of two negative words in one sentence is called a **double negative**. Avoid using **double negatives** because they cancel each other out and make a positive, rather than the negative you meant to use.

Incorrect: We **never** travel **nowhere**.

In this sentence, **never** and **nowhere** are negative words. Used together they form a double negative and confuse the meaning of the sentence. Following are two ways this sentence can be corrected.

Correct: We **never** travel anywhere.

-or-

Correct: We travel **nowhere**.

Incorrect: Jonah **can't** have **no** pie.

Correct: Jonah **can't** have any pie.

-or-

Correct: Jonah can have **no** pie.

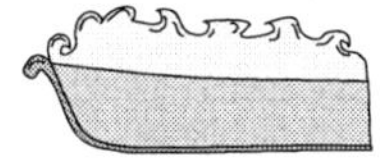

In the incorrect sentence above, both **can't** and **no** are **negatives**. **Can't** is the contraction for **cannot**. Some other negative contractions are **won't**, **don't**, **doesn't**, **aren't**, **hasn't**, **shouldn't**, and **isn't**.

More examples:

Incorrect: My dog **never** forgets **nothing**.

Correct: My dog **never** forgets anything.

-or-

Correct: My dog forgets **nothing**.

Incorrect: You **shouldn't** talk to **nobody**.

Correct: You **shouldn't** talk to anybody.

-or-

Correct: You should talk to **nobody**.

These negative words are adverbs. Remember, on a sentence diagram, an adverb is placed on a slanted line under the verb it describes.

Mariam did **not** sing.

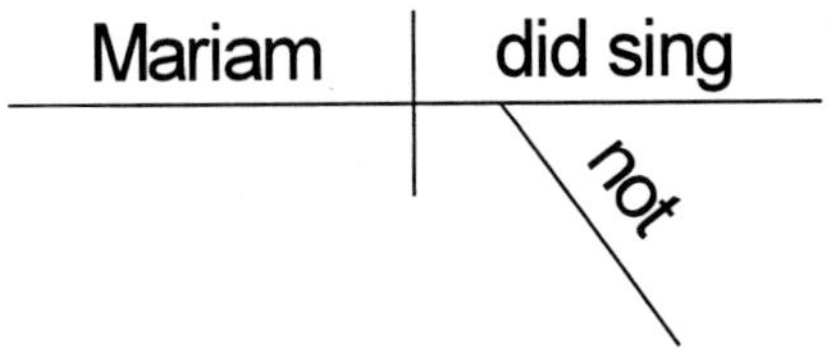

Mariam	did sing
	not

6.7 Synonyms and Antonyms

A **synonym** is a word that has the same or almost the same meaning as another word.

huge gigantic large enormous big

All of these words are **synonyms**. They can be used in place of each other because they each have similar meaning.

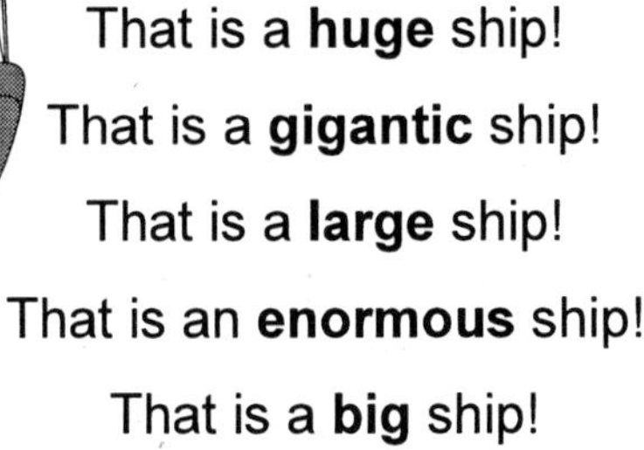

That is a **huge** ship!

That is a **gigantic** ship!

That is a **large** ship!

That is an **enormous** ship!

That is a **big** ship!

All of these sentences have the same meaning.

More examples of synonyms:

This painting is **beautiful**. → This painting is **gorgeous**.

Thank you for the **gift**. → Thank you for the **present**.

The **small** dog barked. → The **little** dog barked.

Please don't **shout**. → Please don't **yell**.

An **antonym** is a word that has the opposite meaning of another word.

clean

dirty **soiled** **filthy** **grimy** **messy**

The words in bold are **antonyms** of the word **clean**. They mean the opposite.

This shirt is **clean**.

This shirt is **dirty**.

These sentences have the opposite meaning.

More examples of antonyms:

walk / jog	long / brief
lost / found	awake / asleep
inside / outside	give / receive
pull / push	same / different
giggle / sob	empty / full
long / short	early / late
excellent / terrible	whisper / scream

6.8 Homonyms

A **homonym** is a word that sounds the same as another word but has a different spelling and meaning.

to too two

The words **to**, **too**, and **two** are **homonyms**. Although they sound the same, they have different meanings.

Are you going **to** the store?

We are going **too**.

I'm bringing my **two** sisters.

The bold words in these sentences sound the same but do not have the same meaning.

More examples of homonyms:

seen / scene	our / hour
brake / break	son / sun
your / you're	scent / sent / cent
dew / do / due	flew / flu
write / right	here / hear
blew / blue	close / clothes

knead / need

pare / pear / pair

lone / loan

seize / seas

wood / would

acts / ax

great / grate

die / dye

deer / dear

there / their / they're

earn / urn

bear / bare

fare / fair

bawl / ball

knot / not

road / rode

6.9 Using Good and Well

Good and **well** are two words that can be easily confused.

Good is an adjective and should be used to describe a noun. Never use it after an action verb.

That was a **good** movie.

Are those your **good** shoes?

In these sentences, **good** is being used to describe the nouns **movie** and **shoes**.

More examples:

That was a **good** cheeseburger.

We did a **good** job on our tests.

Make sure you wear your **good** clothes.

Did you have a **good** day?

Well can be used after an action verb. When it is, it is an adverb and tells **how** something is done.

Incorrect: Sam could not hear good.

Correct: Sam could not hear **well**.

Well is the correct word because it follows the action verb **hear**. It describes **how** Sam hears. Remember that **good** should not be used after an action verb.

More examples:

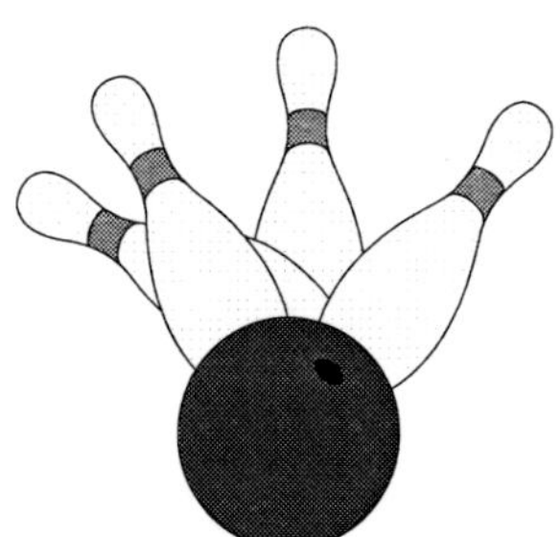

Jeff bowls **well**.

Did you sleep **well**?

The children play **well** together.

Jani doesn't speak **well**.

Well can also be used as an adjective. In this instance, **well** means **healthy** or **not ill**.

Incorrect: Sarah doesn't feel good today.

Correct: Sarah doesn't feel **well** today.

Remember to use **well** rather than **good** when the meaning is **not ill**.

More examples:

I hope you are feeling **well** soon.

Blake is **well** again.

Melissa does not look **well**.

Cari will feel **well** tomorrow.

6.10 Writing a Descriptive Paragraph

A **descriptive paragraph** uses details to describe something or someone. These details help the reader visualize what is being described in the paragraph. When you learn to use descriptive words in your writing, you can make your story come alive for the reader.

Remember, when writing a paragraph, you must first plan what you are going to write. Think of a topic and then make a list of details about the topic.

Example:

Topic→ my eighth birthday

Details: the smell of the food
the taste of the cake
the colorful decorations and presents
the time spent with my friends and family

Think of the order in which you will write the details. Make sure that the order makes sense. Also, make sure that all the details are related to the topic.

Think of a topic sentence that tells the main idea of the paragraph, and then you can write the paragraph using plenty of detail.

Example:

My eighth birthday party was the best party ever. The house was decorated with streamers and balloons in my favorite colors of red, blue, green, and yellow. My mouth watered when I smelled the cheesy hamburgers and the french fries my mother had made for the party. After we ate, it was time to blow out the eight candles on the delicious chocolate cake. Next it was time to open the presents that were wrapped in colorful paper. My favorite part of the celebration was the amazing time I spent with my friends and family.

This paragraph gives a description of the writer's eighth birthday. The sentences describe in detail the party, decorations, food, and fun.

Finally, you should edit your descriptive paragraph. Make sure you indented the first sentence, started all of your sentences with a capital letter, ended each sentence with the correct punctuation, and spelled each word correctly.

Chapter 6 Review

Adverbs: An **adverb** is a word that tells more about a **verb.** Adverbs tell **when**, **where**, or **how** something is done.

Diagramming Adverbs: On a sentence diagram, the **adverb** is placed on a slanted line under the verb it describes.

We sang **today.**

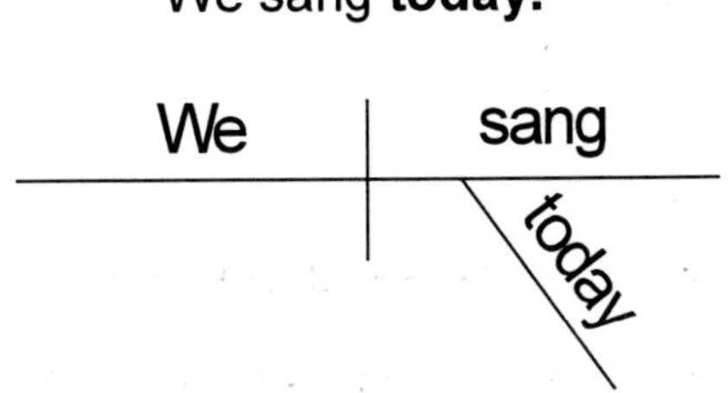

Adverb Placement: In a sentence, an **adverb** can come before or after the verb. Adverbs can be found at the **beginning**, the **middle**, or the **end** of a sentence.

Adverbs that Compare: Many **adverbs** can be used to compare actions. The endings **-er** or **-est** are added to show comparison with most one-syllable adverbs. **More** and **most** are often used with most adverbs of two or more syllables.

-When comparing **two** actions, the ending **-er** is added to most one-syllable adverbs. Add the word **more** before most adverbs of two or more syllables.
-When comparing **three** or **more** actions, the ending **-est** is typically used with most one-syllable adverbs. Add the word **most** before most adverbs of two or more syllables.

-Do not add **-er** to an adverb at the same time you use **more**. Also, do not add **-est** to an adverb at the same time you use **most**.

Relative Pronouns: A **relative pronoun** introduces a group of words, or a clause, that tells more about a **noun**. Words that often act as **relative pronouns** are **who**, **whose**, **which**, and **that**.
Use the relative pronouns **who** and **whose** when referring to people.
Use the relative pronouns **which** and **that** when referring to animals and things.

Relative Adverbs: Like a relative pronoun, a **relative adverb** also introduces a group of words, or a clause, that tells more about a **noun**. Words that often act as **relative adverbs** are **where** , **when**, and **why**.

Double Negatives: A word that means **no** or **not** is called a **negative word**. The words **no**, **not**, **none**, **nothing**, **nowhere**, **neither**, **nobody**, **no one**, and **never** are common negative words. Avoid using double negatives because they cancel each other out and make a positive, rather than the negative you meant to use.

Synonyms and Antonyms: A **synonym** is a word that has the same or almost the same meaning as another word.

An **antonym** is a word that has the opposite meaning of another word.

Homonyms: A **homonym** is a word that sounds the same as another word but has a different spelling and meaning.

Using Good and Well: **Good** and **well** are two words that can be easily confused.
-**Good** is an adjective and can describe only a noun. Do not use it after an action verb.
-**Well** can be used after an action verb. When it is, it is an adverb and tells **how** something is done.
-**Well** can also be used as an adjective. In this instance, **well** means **healthy** or **not ill**.

Chapter 7

Growing with Prepositions

7.1 Prepositions

A **preposition** is a word that shows a relationship between a noun or pronoun and another word in the sentence. The words **at**, **in**, **on**, **from**, and **with** are just a few commonly used prepositions.

We saw Jackson **at** the mall.

Sally went **in** the house.

Place the books **on** the counter.

The bird flew **from** its cage.

I see the moon **with** my binoculars.

The noun or pronoun that follows a preposition is called its **object**. A preposition always has an object. To help locate the object of the preposition, find the preposition and then ask **whom** or **what**.

We saw Jackson **at** the **mall**.

Sally went **in** the **house**.

In the first sentence, the preposition is **at**. At **whom** or at **what**? The object of the preposition is the noun **mall**. In the second sentence, the preposition is **in**. In **whom** or in **what**? The object is **house**.

Sometimes there are other words between the preposition and the noun. Just remember that the noun that answers the question **whom** or **what** is the object of the preposition.

Place the books **on** the short **counter**.

I see the moon **with** my new black **binoculars**.

In the first sentence, the preposition is **on**. On **whom** or on **what**? **Counter** is the object of the preposition. In the second sentence, the preposition is **with**. With **whom** or with **what**? **Binoculars** is the noun that answers this question and is the object of the preposition.

Below is a list of the most commonly used **prepositions**. It is best to memorize this list. Learn one column at a time until you know them all.

Column 1	Column 2	Column 3	Column 4	Column 5
aboard	before	down	of	to
about	behind	during	off	toward
above	below	except	on	under
across	beneath	for	onto	underneath
after	beside	from	out	until
against	between	in	outside	up
along	beyond	inside	over	upon
among	by	into	past	with
around		like	since	within
at		near	through	without
			throughout	

7.2 Prepositional Phrases

A **prepositional phrase** is a group of words that begins with a preposition and ends with the object of the preposition.

The cat is **under the table**.

The eagle flew **across the sky**.

In the first sentence, the preposition is **under**, the object of the preposition is **table**, and the prepositional phrase is **under the table**. In the second sentence, the preposition is **across**, the object of the preposition is **sky**, and the prepositional phrase is **across the sky**.

More examples (with prepositional phrases in bold):

The dog ran **behind the tree**.

Jacob is **on the basketball team**.

The book is **near the counter**.

Ariel jumped **into the pool**.

A prepositional phrase may be two words, or it may be more than two words. When there are words between the preposition and its object, those words are adjectives that modify the object of the preposition.

The fly buzzed **around me**.

Johanna sat **under the old tree**.

In the first sentence, the prepositional phrase has only the two words **around me**. There are no adjectives in this prepositional phrase. In the second sentence, the prepositional phrase has four words. **Under** is the preposition, **tree** is the object of the preposition, and **the old** are adjectives modifying **tree**.

After you find the prepositional phrase, the main sentence parts are easier to find. The subject, verb, direct object, or predicate noun will **never** be found in a prepositional phrase.

The children **in the house** ate dinner.

The	children	in the house	ate	dinner.
↑	↑	↑	↑	↑
Adjective	**Subject**	**Prepositional Phrase**	**Verb**	**Direct Object**

Prepositional phrases can be located at the **beginning**, **middle**, or **end** of a sentence.

After the race we went home.

The coat **in the closet** is mine.

We read **about a medieval castle**.

7.3 Prepositional Phrase Used as an Adjective

A prepositional phrase can sometimes act like an adjective by describing a noun or pronoun. An **adjective phrase** is a prepositional phrase that describes the noun or pronoun it follows by telling **what kind** or **which one**.

Adjective: The **corner** house is mine.

Adjective Phrase: The house **on the corner** is mine.

In these examples, you can see that an adjective phrase functions in the same way that an adjective does. In the first sentence, **corner** is an **adjective** describing the noun **house**. In the second sentence, **on the corner** is an **adjective phrase** describing the noun **house**.

To determine if a prepositional phrase is an adjective phrase, see if it answers the question **what kind** or **which one**.

The girl **in the photograph** is my friend.

A rabbit **with gray fur** ate my carrots.

In the first sentence, **in the photograph** is an adjective phrase because it tells **which one** about the noun **girl**. In the second sentence, **with gray fur** is an adjective phrase because it tells **what kind** about the noun **rabbit**.

More examples:

What kind? We have a *car* **with red paint.**

↑ **Noun** ↑ **Adjective Phrase**

Which one? The *dog* **near the tree** bites!

↑ **Noun** ↑ **Adjective Phrase**

7.4 Prepositional Phrase Used as an Adverb

Just as a prepositional phrase can act like an adjective, it can also act like an adverb. An **adverb phrase** is a prepositional phrase that describes a verb by telling **how**, **when**, or **where**.

Adverb: He fought **bravely**.

Adverb Phrase: He fought **with great bravery**.

In these examples, you can see that an adverb phrase functions in the same way that an adverb does. In the first sentence, **bravely** is an **adverb** describing the verb **fought**. In the second sentence, **with great bravery** is an **adverb phrase** describing the verb **fought**.

To determine if a prepositional phrase is an adverb phrase, see if it answers the question **how**, **when**, or **where**.

She eats **with great eagerness**.

In the morning my grandmother arrived.

We waited **inside the house**.

In the first sentence, **with great eagerness** is an adverb phrase because it tells **how** about the verb **eats**. In the second sentence, **in the morning** is an adverb phrase because it tells **when** about the verb **arrived**. In the third sentence, **inside the house** is an adverb phrase because it tells **where** about the verb **waited**.

As you can see from the above examples, the adverb phrase can be located at the beginning or the end of the sentence.

More examples:

How? Julia *paints* **with great talent**.

↑ **Verb** ↑ **Adverb Phrase**

When? **After our nap** we *played*.

↑ **Adverb Phrase** ↑ **Verb**

Where? The kite *flew* **over the house**.

↑ **Verb** ↑ **Adverb Phrase**

7.5 Diagramming Prepositional Phrases

On a sentence diagram, a prepositional phrase is placed below the word it describes. There are a few steps to follow to diagram a prepositional phrase properly.

First, find the **prepositional phrase** and underline it.

The cat eats <u>under the table</u>.

Next, diagram the rest of the sentence. Leave the prepositional phrase for later.

The cat eats <u>under the table</u>.

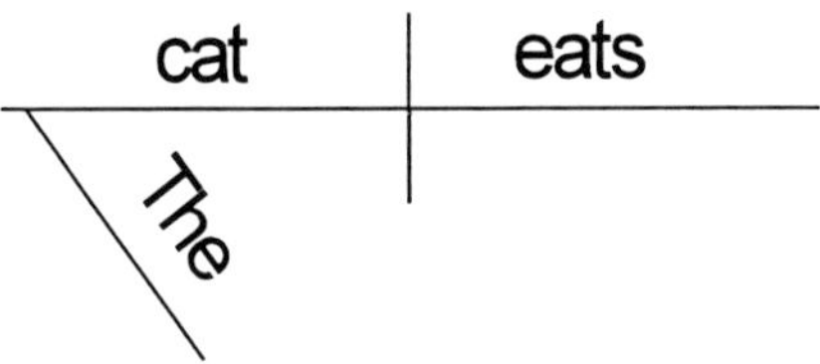

Then, decide if the prepositional phrase is an adjective phrase or an adverb phrase. Remember, adjective phrases tell **what kind** or **which one** about a noun or pronoun. Adverb phrases tell **how**, **when**, or **where** about a verb.

The prepositional phrase **under the table** answers **where** about the **verb**. It is an **adverb phrase** and will be placed under the verb, similar to an adverb.

The **preposition** is placed on a diagonal line below the word it describes.

The cat eats **under** the table.

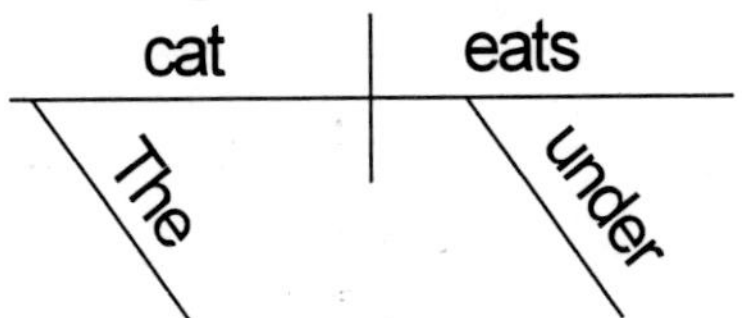

The **object of the preposition** is placed on a horizontal line attached to it.

The cat eats under the **table**.

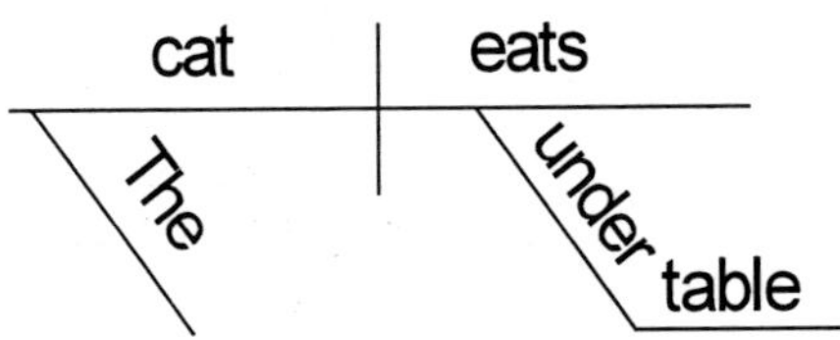

The is a **modifier,** and modifiers of the object of the preposition are placed on diagonal lines below the object.

The cat eats under **the** table.

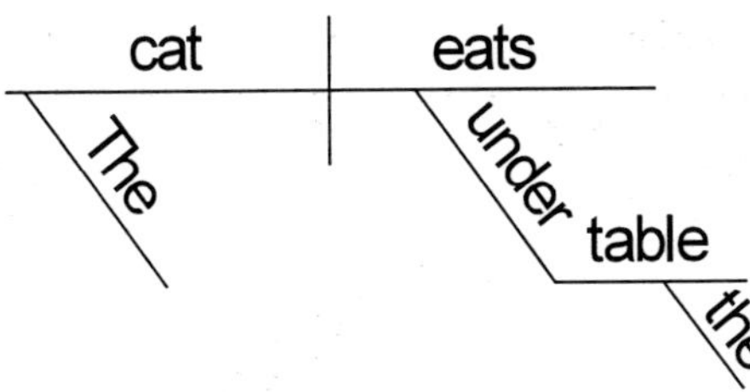

An **adjective phrase** would be placed below the **noun** or **pronoun** it describes, similar to an adjective.

The dog near the tree bites.

In this sentence, the prepositional phrase **near the tree** tells **which one** about the noun **dog**.

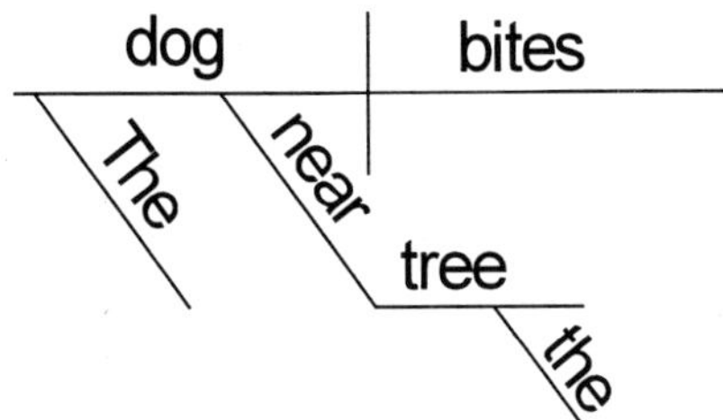

More examples:

After our nap we played.

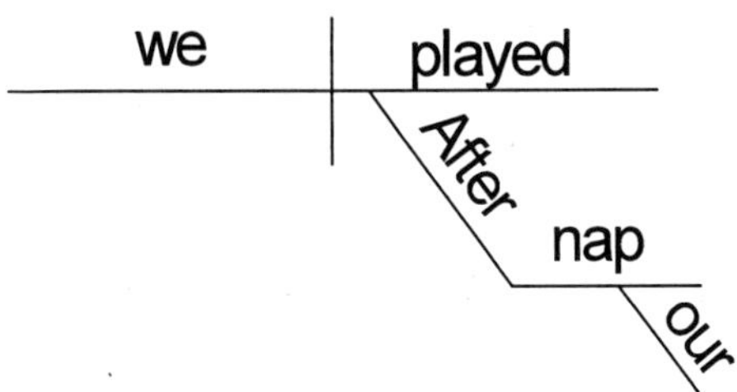

A rabbit with gray fur ate my carrots.

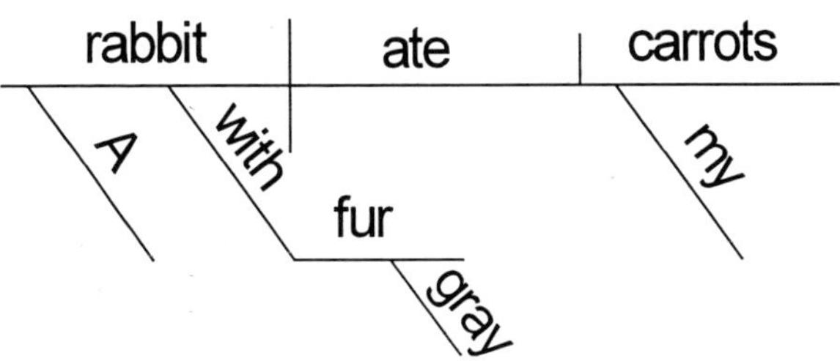

7.6 Preposition or Adverb

Sometimes it is difficult to tell prepositions and adverbs apart. Many words that can be used as prepositions can also be used as adverbs.

Adverb: The bicycle fell **down**.

In this sentence, the word **down** is an **adverb** telling **where** about the verb **fell**.

Preposition: The bicycle fell **down the hill**.

In this sentence, **down** is a **preposition** and **down the hill** is a **prepositional phrase**. We know this because **down** is followed by the noun **hill**. **Hill** is the **object of the preposition**. Only prepositions have objects. Adverbs never have objects. Therefore, **down the hill** is an **adverb phrase** telling **where** about the verb **fell**.

More examples:

Adverb: The insect crawled **up**.

(**Up** is used here as an **adverb**, modifying the **verb crawled**.)

Preposition: The insect crawled **up the wall**.

(**Up** is used here as a **preposition**, and **wall** is its **object**.)

Adverb: The sky darkened **above**.

(**Above** is used here as an **adverb**, modifying the **verb darkened**.)

Preposition: The sky darkened **above the trees**.

(**Above** is used here as a **preposition**, and **trees** is its **object**.)

Adverb: Paulo came **in**.

(**In** is used here as an **adverb**, modifying the **verb came**.)

Preposition: Paulo came **in the house**.

(**In** is used here as a **preposition**, and **house** is its **object**.)

7.7 Building Sentences with Prepositional Phrases

Prepositional phrases can add details to sentences and make them more interesting.

Without Prepositions: The fans cheer.

With Prepositions: The fans **near the sidelines** cheer.

The fans cheer **during the game**.

The first sentence is a complete sentence, but it does not give a lot of detail. The second and third sentences give details by adding the prepositional phrases **near the sidelines** and **during the game**.

More examples:

Without Prepositions: The child cried.

With Prepositions: The child **with brown hai**r cried.

The child cried **after he fell**.

Without Prepositions: A man painted a mural.

With Prepositions: A man **across the room** painted a mural.

On the wall a man painted a mural.

Without Prepositions: The story is terrifying.

With Prepositions: The story **about the forest** is terrifying.

The story is terrifying **in the dark**.

Without Prepositions: The boy dropped a glass.

With Prepositions: The boy **near the stove** dropped a glass.

The boy dropped a glass **under the table**.

You can also use two **prepositional phrases** in the same sentence.

Examples:

Without prepositions: The fans cheer.

With two prepositional phrases: The fans **near the sidelines** cheer **during the game**.

Without prepositions: The child cried.

With two prepositional phrases: The child **with brown hair** cried **after he fell**.

Without prepositions: The boy dropped a glass.

With two prepositional phrases: The boy **near the stove** dropped a glass **under the table**.

7.8 Conjunctions

A **conjunction** is a word used to join words, phrases, or sentences. Three conjunctions are **and**, **but**, and **or**. Each conjunction has a special job. However, unlike prepositions, conjunctions do not show relationships. They just connect words.

The conjunction **and** adds one item to another.

The gift has red paper **and** a blue bow.

Kristin has blue eyes **and** brown hair.

The conjunction **but** contrasts one item with another.

I like peas **but** not broccoli.

Andrew reads comic books **but** writes poetry.

The conjunction **or** shows a choice between one item and another.

Would you like to go to the movies **or** stay home?

You can fold the laundry **or** put it away.

A **conjunction** can be used to join two or more simple subjects that have the same predicate into a **compound subject**.

David ate steak. Eddie ate steak.

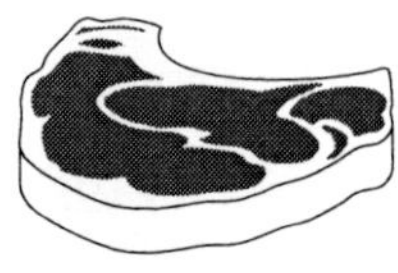

David **and** Eddie ate steak.

More examples:

The bird **and** the dog are in the house.

Quinn **or** Jasper will help you.

My sister Chloe **and** my cousin Lia went sledding.

A **conjunction** can be used to join two or more verbs that have the same subject into a **compound predicate**.

Pilar wrote the letter. Pilar mailed the letter.

↓

Pilar wrote **and** mailed the letter.

More examples:

Tommy picked **and** ate the tomatoes.

Hector folded the clothes **and** put them away.

We might watch a parade **or** ride the roller coaster.

A **conjunction** can be used to join two or more simple sentences into a **compound sentence**. Use a comma to separate sentences joined with **and**, **but**, or **or.**

John wrote a story. His sister read it.

↓

John wrote a story**, and** his sister read it.

More examples:

We can eat the apples**, or** we can make applesauce.

Tina would like to go**, but** she is tired.

Jenn dug up the garden**, and** Greg planted the seeds.

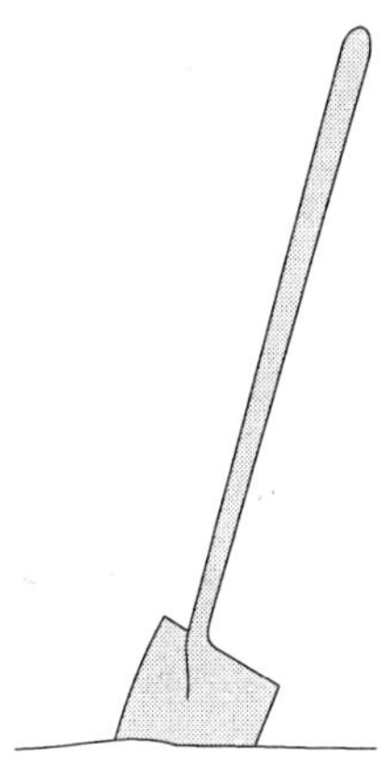

7.9 Interjections

An **interjection** is a word or a group of words that expresses strong feeling or emotion. Interjections usually occur at the beginning of a sentence. Strong interjections are followed by an exclamation mark. They can show different types of feelings, such as surprise, pain, fear, joy, and disgust.

Surprise: **Wow!** What a great gift!

Pain: **Ouch!** That hurts!

Fear: **Yikes!** You scared me!

Joy: **Hurray!** I won the race!

Disgust: **Well!** That was rude!

An interjection never has a subject. Also, notice that an interjection is set off from the rest of the sentence by a punctuation mark. The first word after the strong interjection and its punctuation mark, an exclamation point, is capitalized.

Some interjections are followed by a comma. These are called mild interjections.

Hey, you scored a goal!

Darn, it's raining!

My, that's a beautiful dress!

Whew, that was a close call!

Oh, we are going to be late!

A comma sets off the mild interjection from the rest of the sentence. The first word after the mild interjection is not capitalized.

7.10 Of and Have

Do not make the mistake of using the preposition **of** in place of the verb **have**.

Incorrect: I should of eaten that orange.

Correct: I should **have** eaten that orange.

Could of, **should of**, and **would of** should **not** be used. These are incorrect uses of the word **of**. The correct constructions are **could have**, **should have**, and **would have**.

The incorrect usage of the word **of** is probably based on the misunderstanding of the spoken contractions "**could've**" (could have), "**should've**" (should have), and "**would've**" (would have).

More examples:

Incorrect: You should of gone to bed earlier.

Correct: You should **have** gone to bed earlier.

Incorrect: Dad would of liked that pizza.

Correct: Dad would **have** liked that pizza.

Incorrect: They should of finished the job by now.

Correct: They should **have** finished the job by now.

Incorrect: He could of mowed the lawn today.

Correct: He could **have** mowed the lawn today.

7.11 Writing a Book Report

A **book report** is something you write to let others know your opinion about a book you have read. This will help others decide whether they want to read the book.

Certain elements are always included in a book report. You should start with an **introduction**, which is a paragraph that includes the author's name and the title of the book. Book titles should be underlined. Also include a brief description of the type of book. Is it an adventure, fantasy, mystery, biography, fiction, or nonfiction story?

Next write a paragraph providing some **details** of the book. Tell about the setting of the book. Where and when did it happen? Discuss the main characters and give a brief description of each one. Describe the plot briefly without giving too much information.

Finally, write a paragraph that includes your **opinion** of the book. Did you like it or dislike it? Provide reasons and examples.

Example: *(Written by Jacob age 9)*

The Borrowers by Mary Norton is a fiction book about a family of tiny people living under the floor of a kitchen. This story tells about how they live and try to never be seen. It also tells how they borrow what they need from the people who live in the house.

This story takes place under a clock in an old house in England. Pod Clock is the father borrower. He does all of the borrowing for the family. Homily Clock is the mother and she never wants to leave her home under the kitchen. Arietty Clock is the daughter who is bored and lonely and wants to find out what is in the house above. She loves to read.

I loved this book because it was exciting. I loved when Arietty met the boy under the tree. I was worried that they would have to move after she was seen. The book is also funny. The last name of the borrowers depends on where they live in the house. The Clock family lives under the clock. The Overmantles lived over the mantle. I would recommend this book to anybody who likes adventure.

Chapter 7 Review

Prepositions: A **preposition** is a word that shows a relationship between a noun or pronoun and another word in the sentence. The noun or pronoun that follows the preposition is called its **object**. A preposition always has an object.

Sometimes there are other words between the preposition and the noun. To help find the object of the preposition, find the preposition and then ask **whom** or **what**. The noun that answers this question is the object of the preposition.

Below is a list of the most commonly used **prepositions**.

aboard	before	down	of	to
about	behind	during	off	toward
above	below	except	on	under
across	beneath	for	onto	underneath
after	beside	from	out	until
against	between	in	outside	up
along	beyond	inside	over	upon
among	by	into	past	with
around		like	since	within
at		near	through	without
			throughout	

Prepositional Phrases: A **prepositional phrase** is a group of words that begins with a preposition and ends with the object of the preposition.

A prepositional phrase may be two words, or it may be more than two words. When there are words between the preposition and its object, those words are adjectives that modify the object of the preposition. Prepositional phrases can be located at the **beginning**, **middle**, or **end** of a sentence.

Prepositional Phrase Used as an Adjective: A prepositional phrase can sometimes act like an adjective by describing a noun or pronoun. An **adjective phrase** is a prepositional phrase that describes the noun or pronoun it follows by telling **what kind** or **which one**.

Prepositional Phrase Used as an Adverb: Just as a prepositional phrase can act like an adjective, it can also act like an adverb. An **adverb phrase** is a prepositional phrase that describes a verb by telling **how**, **when**, or **where**.

Diagramming Prepositional Phrases: On a sentence diagram, a prepositional phrase is placed below the word it describes. First, the **preposition** is placed on a diagonal line below the word it describes. Next, the **object of the preposition** is placed on a horizontal line attached to it. Finally, **modifiers** of the object of the preposition are placed on diagonal lines below the object.

An **adjective phrase** is placed below the **noun** or pronoun it describes.

The dog <u>near the tree</u> bites.

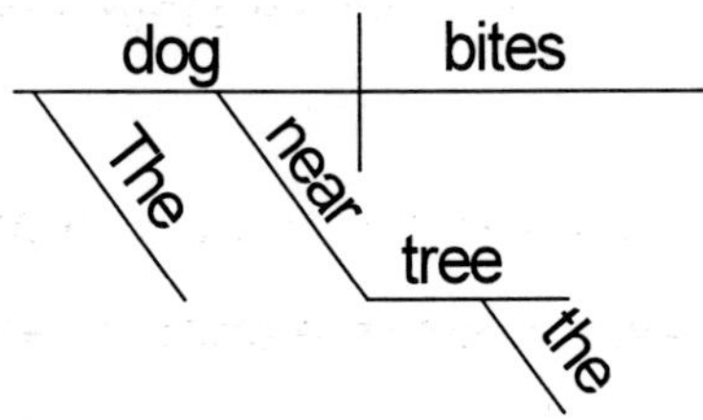

An **adverb** phrase is placed below the **verb** it describes.

The cat eats <u>under the table</u>.

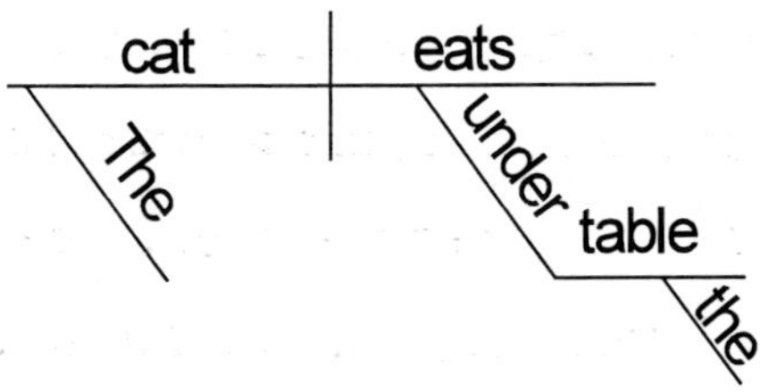

<u>**Preposition or Adverb**</u>: Sometimes it is difficult to tell prepositions and adverbs apart. Depending on how they are used, many prepositions can also be adverbs.

<u>**Conjunctions**</u>: A **conjunction** is a word used to join words, phrases, or sentences. Three conjunctions are **and**, **but**, and **or**.

-The conjunction **and** adds one item to another.
-The conjunction **but** contrasts one item with another.
-The conjunction **or** shows a choice between one item and another.

-A **conjunction** can be used to join two or more simple subjects that have the same predicate into a compound subject.
-A **conjunction** can be used to join two or more verbs that have the same subject into a compound predicate.
-A **conjunction** can be used to join two or more simple sentences into a compound sentence. Use a comma to separate sentences joined with **and**, **but**, or **or.**

Interjections: An **interjection** is a word or a group of words that expresses strong feeling or emotion. Interjections usually occur at the beginning of a sentence. Strong interjections are followed by an exclamation mark. Mild interjections are followed by a comma.

Of and Have: Do not make the mistake of using the preposition **of** in place of the verb **have**. **Could of**, **should of**, and **would of** should **not** be used. The correct constructions are **could have**, **should have**, and **would have**.

Chapter 8

Growing with Words and Punctuation

8.1 Prefixes

A **prefix** is a word part added to the **beginning** of a base word to make a new word. Prefixes usually change the meaning of the word.

The spelling of the root word remains the same when a prefix is added. Some prefixes are **im-**, **dis-**, and **pre-**.

The prefix **im-** means **not.**

im + perfect = **im**perfect

im + polite = **im**polite

The prefix **im-** with the base word **perfect** means **not perfect**. The prefix **im-** with the base word **polite** means **not polite.**

More examples:

immature = not mature

impersonal = not personal

improper = not proper

impatient = not patient

The prefix **dis-** means **not**.

dis + honest = **dis**honest

dis + satisfied = **dis**satisfied

The prefix **dis-** with the base word **honest** means **not honest**. The prefix **dis-** with the base word **satisfied** means **not satisfied**.

More examples:

disagreeable = not agreeable **dis**like = not like

disrespectful = not respectful **dis**obey = not obey

The prefix **pre-** means **before**.

pre + arrange = **pre**arrange

pre + cook = **pre**cook

The prefix **pre-** with the base word **arrange** means **arrange before**. The prefix **pre-** with the base word **cook** means **cook before**.

More examples:

precaution = caution before **pre**heat = heat before

prepackage = package before **pre**pay = pay before

8.2 Rise and Raise

Rise and **raise** are often confused.

Rise means **to go up** or **to get up without help**. **Rise** is **never** followed by a direct object.

The sun will **rise** soon.

The balloon **rises** in the sky.

Harry is **rising** from his seat.

The smoke has **risen** into the sky.

In these sentences, the forms of **rise** do not have a direct object. The sun, the balloon, Harry, and smoke **rise** without help.

Incorrect: Hot air balloons **raise** in the air.

Correct: Hot air balloons **rise** in the air.

Incorrect: The farmer **raises** early to feed the animals.

Correct: The farmer **rises** early to feed the animals.

Incorrect: The crowd is **raising** to sing the song.

Correct: The crowd is **rising** to sing the song.

Incorrect: The boy has **raised** from his bed.

Correct: The boy has **risen** from his bed.

Raise means **to lift**, **to increase**, or **to grow with help**. **Raise** is always followed by a direct object because there is always some object that is being raised, or lifted.

Raise the curtain and look out the window.

Ethan **raises** his hand to ask a question.

We are **raising** tomatoes in our garden.

Uncle Fred has **raised** pigs on his farm.

In these sentences, the direct objects are **curtain**, **hand**, **tomatoes**, and **pigs**. They receive the action of the verb **raise**.

Incorrect: My grandmother always **rises** vegetables.
Correct: My grandmother always **raises** vegetables.

Incorrect: The store will **rise** its prices.
Correct: The store will **raise** its prices.

Incorrect: The skunk is **rising** its tail!
Correct: The skunk is **raising** its tail!

Incorrect: I have **risen** enough money for my trip.
Correct: I have **raised** enough money for my trip.

Remember, something can **rise** by itself, but external help is needed to **raise** something.

8.3 Let and Leave

Use the word **let** to mean **to allow** or **to permit**.

Please **let** me have another bowl of soup.

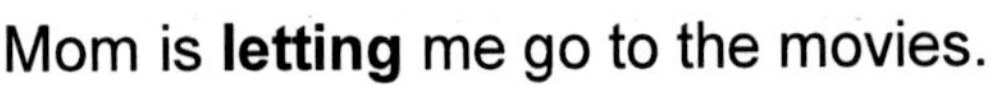

Mom is **letting** me go to the movies.

I hope Bob **lets** me sit next to him.

In these sentences, the word **let** and its different forms mean **to allow** or **to permit**.

Allow me have another bowl of soup.

Mom is **permitting** me go to the movies.

I hope Bob **allows** me sit next to him.

Incorrect: **Leave** me come with you!
Correct: **Let** me come with you!

Incorrect: Alex is **leaving** the dog into the house.
Correct: Alex is **letting** the dog into the house.

Incorrect: Grandma **leaves** us stay up late.
Correct: Grandma **lets** us stay up late.

Use the word **leave** to mean **to go away** or **depart from**. It also means **allow to remain**.

Did Karen **leave** the house?

I hope he **leaves** me alone.

Will you be **leaving** with Troy?

In these sentences, the word **leave** and its different forms mean **to go away** or **depart from** and **allow to remain**.

Did Karen **depart from** the house?

I hope he **allows** me **to remain** alone.

Will you be **going away** with Troy?

Incorrect: We will **let** as soon as possible.
Correct: We will **leave** as soon as possible.

Incorrect: She always **lets** her umbrella at home.
Correct: She always **leaves** her umbrella at home.

Incorrect: I will be **letting** your gift on the counter.
Correct: I will be **leaving** your gift on the counter.

8.4 Lend and Borrow

Sometimes the verbs **lend** and **borrow** are confused. **Lend** and **borrow** have similar meanings and can be easily confused.

I will **lend** my book to you.

You may **borrow** a book from me.

The word **lend** means **to give someone else something** for a short period of time with the expectation that it will be returned.

If you are cold Sherri can **lend** you a sweater.

This sentence means that Sherri will **give** the sweater to you **for a short period of time**.

Incorrect: Are you **borrowing** your tools to John?
Correct: Are you **lending** your tools to John?

Incorrect: The library **borrows** books to people.
Correct: The library **lends** books to people.

Incorrect: Will you **borrow** me your pencil?
Correct: Will you **lend** me your pencil?

The word **borrow** means **to receive something from someone** for a short period of time with the expectation that it will be returned.

May Toby **borrow** your sweater until tomorrow?

This sentence means that Toby will **receive** the sweater **for a short period of time**.

Incorrect: Mary **lends** books from the library.
Correct: Mary **borrows** books from the library.

Incorrect: John is always **lending** tools from Dad.
Correct: John is always **borrowing** tools from Dad.

Incorrect: Did you **lend** my pencil from me?
Correct: Did you **borrow** my pencil from me?

8.5 Teach and Learn

Teach and **learn** are words that are also easily confused.

I will **teach** you how to ride a bike.

You will **learn** how to ride a bike.

The word **teach** means **to give knowledge** or **show someone how to do something**.

Mrs. Grant **teaches** math to the children.

This sentence means that Mrs. Grant will **give knowledge** about math to the children.

Incorrect: Dad **learned** me how to bake a cake.
Correct: Dad **taught** me how to bake a cake.

Incorrect: I am **learning** my dog how to roll over.
Correct I am **teaching** my dog how to roll over.

Incorrect: Did you **learn** him how to tie his shoes?
Correct: Did you **teach** him how to tie his shoes?

The word **learn** means **to get** or **receive knowledge**.

Bobby **learns** math from Mrs. Grant.

This sentence means that Bobby **will receive** knowledge about math from Mrs. Grant.

Incorrect: I **taught** how to bake a cake from Dad.
Correct: I **learned** how to bake a cake from Dad.

Incorrect: My dog is **teaching** how to roll over from me.
Correct: My dog is **learning** how to roll over from me.

Incorrect: Will you ever **teach** to tie your shoes?
Correct: Will you ever **learn** to tie your shoes?

8.6 Troublesome Words

It is easy to confuse the words **to**, **too**, and **two**. They are **homonyms** (review lesson **6.8**), so the three words are spelled differently and have different meanings.

To is a preposition that is often used at the beginning of a prepositional phrase.

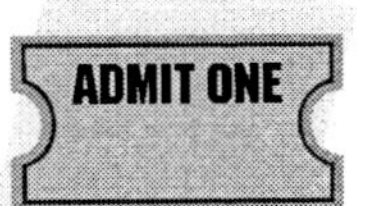

I am going **to a movie**.

Let's go **to the pool**.

Grandma went **to the beauty parlor**.

Too means **also** or **more than enough**.

Did you go to the doctor **too**?

I ate **too** much ice cream.

It is **too** hot in here!

Two is a **number**.

My sister is **two** years old.

We have **two** dogs and one cat.

Our vacation lasted **two** weeks.

They're, **their**, and **there** are also homonyms, so the three words are spelled differently and have different meanings.

They're is a contraction of the words **they are**.

I think **they're** going to be late.

They're best friends.

They're playing checkers.

To make sure you have used **they're** correctly, try replacing **they're** with **they are** in the sentence. If **they are** does not sound right, try another of the homonyms.

Their is a possessive pronoun that means **belonging to them**. **Their** is used to show **ownership**.

Is that **their** cat?

They forgot **their** books.

Their mother is taking us to the library.

There is a word that is used to tell **where**. Also, **there** is often used at to begin a sentence.

I want to go **there**.

There was no room in the suitcase.

Sarah went **there** on her birthday.

8.7 More Troublesome Words

Some words cause trouble because they sound alike. The sets of words **it's/its**, **you're/your**, and **who's/whose** can be confusing for this reason. They sound alike but have different meanings and spellings.

It's is a contraction of the words **it is** or **it has**.

It is a lovely day! → **It's** a lovely day!

I think **it has** fallen over. → I think **it's** fallen over.

More examples:

Dad said **it's** going to snow.

It's time to leave.

I don't think **it's** ever been this cold!

It's too bad Pamela was not home.

To make sure you have used **it's** correctly, try replacing **it's** with **it is** or **it has** in the sentence. If **it is** or **it has** does not sound right, then use **its**.

Its means **belonging to it** and is a possessive pronoun. Use **its** to show ownership. Although the word **its** is possessive, it does not contain an apostrophe.

The cat arched **its** back.

Its name is Fluffy.

Did you see **its** white paws?

Its collar is on the counter.

You're is a contraction of the words **you are**.

I think **you are** funny! → I think **you're** funny!

You are my best friend! → **You're** my best friend.

More examples:

You're doing a wonderful job!

Dan said **you're** interested in science.

You're going to be late!

Are you sure **you're** ready?

To make sure you have used **you're** correctly, try replacing **you're** with **you are** in the sentence. If **you are** does not sound right, then use **your**.

Your means **belonging to you** and is a possessive pronoun. Use **your** to show ownership.

Your mother wants you to go home.

How was **your** day?

Your hair is long.

Is that **your** coat?

Who's is a contraction of the words **who is** or **who has**.

Who is at the door? → **Who's** at the door?

Who has been eating? → **Who's** been eating?

More examples:

I know **who's** been riding my bike.

Who's going with me?

Do you know **who's** on the telephone?

Who's been making a mess?

To make sure you have used **who's** correctly, try replacing **who's** with **who is** or **who has** in the sentence. If **who is** or **who has** does not sound right, then use **whose**.

Whose is the possessive form of the pronoun **who**. Whose means **belonging to whom**. Use **whose** to show ownership.

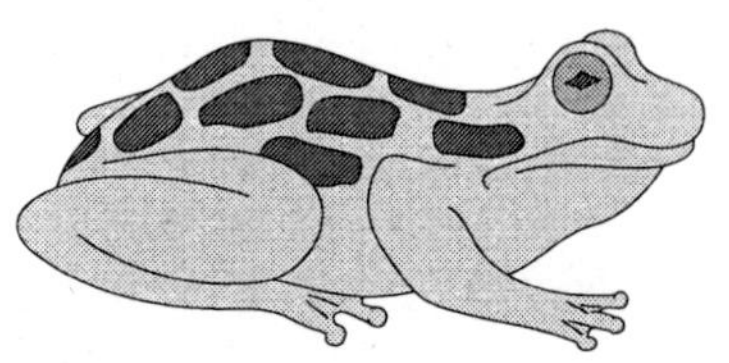

Whose frog is that?

I know **whose** car that is.

Do you know **whose** turn it is?

Whose house are we visiting?

8.8 Abbreviations

An **abbreviation** is a shortened form of a word or phrase. Most abbreviations begin with a capital letter and end with a period. Most dictionaries contain a section of commonly used abbreviations.

Initials are **names** that have been abbreviated. An initial can be used for the first name, middle name, or all parts of a name. Initials are capitalized and followed by a period.

Oliver Jones → **O.** Jones

Axel John Lee → Axel **J.** Lee

Melissa Claire Gregory → **M.C.** Gregory

Pilar Anabella Arroyo → **P.A.A.**

Titles before and after proper names can be abbreviated. They are also capitalized and followed by a period. **Miss** is a title that is not abbreviated, but it is still capitalized.

Jr. → Junior

Sr. → Senior

Mr. → Mister

Mrs. → Mistress

Prof. → Professor

Rev. → Reverend

Atty. → Attorney

Dr. → Doctor

Pres. → President

Sen. → Senator

Sgt. → Sergeant

Capt. → Captain

Geographical terms that come before or after a proper noun can be abbreviated. They are capitalized and followed by a period.

St. → Street

Ave. → Avenue

Hwy. → Highway

Apt. → Apartment

Co. → County

Prov. → Province

Mt. → Mountain

Rd. → Road

Dr. → Drive

Rte. → Route

Bldg. → Building

Dist. → District

Terr. → Territory

Natl. → National

The names of the **50 U.S. states**, **Canadian provinces**, and **territories** can be abbreviated. Two initials are used with no period.

CA → California

IN → Indiana

PA → Pennsylvania

DC → District of Columbia

ON → Ontario

HI → Hawaii

NM → New Mexico

TX → Texas

PR→ Puerto Rico

SK → Saskatchewan

8.9 More Abbreviations

There are common abbreviations for **calendar items**, **time**, and **measurements**. Don't forget to check your dictionary's section of abbreviations for any that are not mentioned here.

The names of the **days of the week** are capitalized and followed by a period when they are abbreviated.

Sun. → Sunday

Mon. → Monday

Tues. → Tuesday

Wed. → Wednesday

Thurs. → Thursday

Fri. → Friday

Sat. → Saturday

Most of the names of the **months of the year** can be abbreviated. They are capitalized and followed by a period. **May**, **June**, and **July** are rarely abbreviated.

Jan. → January

Feb. → February

Mar. → March

Apr. → April

Aug. → August

Sept. → September

Oct. → October

Nov. → November

Dec. → December

Other calendar items can be abbreviated.

yr. → year

mo. → month

The abbreviations of **time before noon** and **after noon** can be written with capital or lowercase letters, each followed by a period.

A.M. or **a.m.** → before noon
P.M. or **p.m.** → after noon

There are abbreviations for **clock times**. They are not capitalized, but they are followed by a period.

sec. → second

hr. → hour

min. → minute

There are also abbreviations for **units of measure**.

in. → inch

ft. → foot

yd. → yard

mi. → mile

pt. → pint

qt. → quart

oz. → ounce

lb. → pound

gal. → gallon

doz. → dozen

tsp. → teaspoon

tbsp. → tablespoon

8.10 Commas

Place a comma after the name of the person to whom you are speaking in a sentence. As we discussed in lesson **2.9**, this is called a **noun of direct address**.

Nouns of direct address are set off by commas no matter where they are located in the sentence. They may be at the **beginning**, in the **middle**, or at the **end** of the sentence.

Mom, I hurt my hand.

I think**, David,** that you should sit down.

How old are you**, Thora**?

Place a comma after **yes**, **no**, or **well** when it is used as a mild interjection (review lesson **7.9**).

Yes, Diego is coming with us.

No, she does not know the answer.

Well, I think you did a great job!

A comma is used to separate words or groups of **words in a series**. In a series of three or more items, use a comma after each item except the last. This means that the number of commas will be one fewer than the number of items.

Robin, John, and **Nick** rode the rollercoaster.
(three items/proper nouns and two commas)

The children **laughed, sang, danced,** and **played**.
(four items/verbs and three commas)

Place a comma before **and**, **but**, or **or** in a **compound sentence**.

My uncle loves to cook**, but** my aunt loves to bake.

The dog barked**, and** the cat climbed the tree.

Use a comma to separate the parts of a **street address** or a **geographic location**, for example, the name of a **town** or **city** and its **state**. A comma is placed after the state unless it is the last word in the sentence.

Raleigh, North Carolina, is a beautiful city.

We are moving to 123 Fifth Avenue, Chicago, Illinois.

Set off the parts of a **date** with commas. Also, when a date is given in a sentence, place a comma after the year unless the date comes at the end of the sentence.

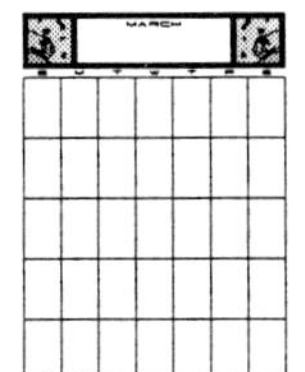

Saturday**,** March 11**,** 2006

I was born on January 23**,** 1964.

On September 21**,** 1996**,** my parents were married.

Place a comma after the **greeting** in a friendly letter.

Dear Jessica**,**

Dear Uncle George**,**

Place a comma after the **closing** in a letter.

Sincerely**,**

Yours truly**,**

Your friend**,**

Chapter 8 Review

Prefixes: A **prefix** is a word part added to the **beginning** of a base word to make a new word. Prefixes usually change the meaning of the word.

-The prefix **im-** means **not.**

-The prefix **dis-** can mean **not**.

-The prefix **pre-** means **before**.

Rise and Raise: **Rise** means **to go up** or **to get up without help**. **Rise** is **never** followed by a direct object. **Raise** means **to lift**, **to increase**, or **to grow with help**. **Raise** is always followed by a direct object.

Let and Leave: Use the word **let** to mean **to allow** or **to permit**. Use the word **leave** to mean **to go away** or **depart from**. It also means **allow to remain**.

Lend and Borrow: The word **lend** means **to give someone else something** for a short period of time with the expectation that it will be returned. The word **borrow** means **to receive something from someone** for a short period of time with the expectation that it will be returned.

<u>**Teach and Learn**</u>: The word **teach** means **to give knowledge** or **show someone how to do something**. The word **learn** means **to get** or **receive knowledge**.

<u>**Troublesome Words**</u>: Do not confuse the homonyms **to**, **too**, and **two**. **To** is a preposition that is often used at the beginning of a prepositional phrase. **Too** means **also** or **more than enough**. **Two** is a **number**.

They're, **their**, and **there** are also homonyms. **They're** is a contraction of the words **they are**. **Their** is a possessive pronoun that means **belonging to them** and is used to show **ownership**.
There is a word that is used to tell **where** and is often used at the beginning of a sentence.

Some words cause trouble because they sound alike. The sets of words **it's/its**, **you're/your**, and **who's/whose** can be confusing for this reason.

It's is a contraction of the words **it is** or **it has**.
Its means **belonging to it** and is a possessive pronoun used to show ownership. Notice that although the word **its** is possessive, it does not contain an apostrophe.

You're is a contraction of the words **you are**.

Your is a possessive pronoun meaning **belonging to you** and is used to show ownership.

Who's is a contraction of the words **who is** or **who has**. **Whose** is the possessive form of the pronoun **who**. **Whose** means **belonging to whom**.

<u>**Abbreviations**</u>: An **abbreviation** is a shortened form of a word or phrase. Most abbreviations begin with a capital letter and end with a period.

-**Initials** are **names** that have been abbreviated.

-**Titles** before and after proper names can be abbreviated.

-**Geographical terms** that come before or after a proper noun can be abbreviated.

-The names of the **50 U.S. states**, **Canadian provinces**, and **territories** can be abbreviated.

-The names of the **days of the week** are capitalized and followed by a period when they are abbreviated.

- Most of the names of the **months of the year** can be abbreviated.

-The abbreviations of **time before noon** and **after noon** can be written with capital or lowercase letters, each followed by a period.

-There are abbreviations for **units of measure**.

-There are abbreviations for **clock times**.

Commas:

-**Nouns of direct address** are set off by commas no matter where they are in the sentence.

-Place a comma after **yes**, **no**, or **well** at the beginning of a sentence.

- A comma is used to separate words or groups of **words in a series**. In a series of three or more items, use a comma after each item except the last. This means that the number of commas that should be used in a series is one fewer than the number of items.

-Place a comma before **and**, **but**, or **or** in a **compound sentence**.

-Use a comma to separate the parts of a street address or a geographic location, for example, the name of a **town** or **city** and its **state**.

-Set off the parts of a **date** with commas.

-Place a comma after the **greeting** in a friendly letter.

-Place a comma after the **closing** in a letter.

<This page intentionally left blank>